D1622149

INNER COMMUNION

INNER
COMMUNION

Sondra Ray

Celestial Arts
Berkeley, California

A NOTE ON THE COVER ART

The beautiful color art on the cover is a "yantra." A yantra is a cosmic diagram. What the mantra is in the space of sound, the yantra is in the space of vision. This particular yantra is found in the holy temple shrine of Badrinath in the Himalayas in India. This yantra is said to be drawn by the Mother Parvati herself to give protection to her husband Shiva when engaged in severe penance.

—by Harigovind

Introduction copyright (c) 1990 by Robert Coon.

Copyright (c) 1990 by Sondra Ray.

All rights reserved. No part of this book may be reproduced in any form, except for brief review, without the written permission of the publisher.

CELESTIAL ARTS
P.O. Box 7327
Berkeley, California

Cover art by Philip Tarlow
Cover design by Ken Scott
Text design and composition by Hal Hershey

Library of Congress Card Catalog Number: 90-82187
ISBN 0-89087-621-5

First Printing, 1990

0 9 8 7 6 5 4 3 2 1
94 93 92 91 90

Manufactured in the United States of America

My special thanks to
ROBERT COON
DAVID SPANGLER
and
HEART-MASTER DA LOVE-ANANDA

Dedication

Although unplanned by me, I am certain that it is no mistake that I began this book on Easter Sunday and finished it on Christmas Day. I acknowledge the Christ Consciousness and the blessings of Babaji for this work; however, I especially want to dedicate this book to:

THE DIVINE MOTHER

The Great Goddess, matrix and creatrix of all that is, who takes many forms or aspects of manifestation; and especially to the form of the BLESSED VIRGIN MARY, now appearing to the visionaries in Yugoslavia.

It is in her honor that I write this book to glorify her; and thank her for calling me and allowing me in; so that I may humbly share her blessings, her energy, and especially her message with you now.

OH, QUEEN OF PEACE, I BOW TO YOU.

Contents

INTRODUCTION

The Chalice of Life

by Robert Coon

Sondra Ray is a pioneer upon the High Way of Divine Life. I have observed her spiritual journey with great interest for several years now. On special occasions, our individual Ways have intersected and communed within profound densities of Life and Joy. We were both guided to celebrate Harmonic Convergence, 17th August, 1987, here at Glastonbury, England—the Planetary Heart Chakra. I am certain that our Pathways shall cross in Service to the Divine on many occasions as we travel deeper into the Heartland of the New Aeon which is now unfolding. May each such crossway Anoint the Lord of Life within every Being.

As we enter the 1990s, I perceive that Sondra is entering a very important phase of her personal journey. The challenges, purifications and initiations of Bodhisattvahood are beginning to manifest frequently and visibly within Sondra's experience of Living and Serving upon this earth. This business of becoming a Bodhisattva is a very tricky one! Especially here in the West. I wish Sondra every success within the birth-chambers of this initiation.

Within the Spiritual Order that I am a member of, the A.A., the Bodhisattva is known as The Master of the

3

Grail. Here we connect with the title and the central theme of the book you hold in your hands—Sondra Ray's *Inner Communion*. For the Bodhisattva is a woman or a man who has managed to remove all limitations of ego from Self so that there is no inner resistance to either receiving or giving the Communion of the Holy Grail. When we have removed all resistance to giving and receiving from our Wills, our Minds, our Hearts, then the Richness of True Communion begins to be experienced in every situation. There are five degrees of Initiation beyond the Master of the Grail—the Bodhisattva. Through each of these five degrees, the Magick of Divine Communion becomes deeper, more creative, and more expansive. In the final stages of this process, all resistance to the Communion of Total and Infinite Life is abolished from the physical Body. This is the Christing of Flesh—the attainment of Physical Immortality, where the alchemical Wedding of Body and Spirit is consummated. Through Total Communion, the Triumph of Life is Complete.

Illusions are parasites dependent upon dualities. Dualities are not real. At the Heart of Communion, Immortal Transformation—complete Union with the Divine—occurs, and all dualities and all illusions vanish. Only the Eternal Joy of Radiant Truth remains ... The Word is made Flesh ... You and the Father-Mother are forever and ever One.

In Service to the Theme of this Book, I would like to devote the pages of this introduction to an exploration of the Magick of Communion. Let us breathe together—You and I—in the Here and Now. And Let us invoke—You and I—the Living Spirit of Truth, Here and Now, to Be With Us and to Illuminate the Way of Communion ... Oh Let It Be!

We begin exactly where we are: What can I assume about you here in this instant? You are alive and you are choosing to let the words and thoughts of this book, *Inner Communion*, into your consciousness—into your Life. Here we have the basic conditions needed for Communion. For Communion is always about Life, Choice, and Change. The Art of Communion is Pure Magick, for Magick is the Art of giving birth to Change that is in harmony with your Divine True Will. These Words are Alive—radiant with the Abundance of Immortal Joy ... Feast upon these Words ... And may the Recreation of Christed Life be established throughout thy Flesh!

In the Russian Orthodox Church, the Holy Spirit is invoked to activate the bread and wine. This is a Ritual of essential importance. The conscious and sincere Invocation of the Living Spirit of Truth increases the potency of Divine Grace within every form of Communion. Let us, once again, consider our present situation: In this instant of time, I am writing these words. In this instant of time, you are reading them. Through Communion, our experiences are transcending linear time. In Eternity, the mutual interchange of all experience is complete and simultaneous at all times. The Divine knows your needs before you ask—but you still need to ask! The Invocation of the Holy Spirit is the most effective way to do this asking.

If the white wafer used in many Christian Churches can act as the Body or Flesh of Christ, surely any object can. These wafers contain no nutrition and look like they are made out of plastic. The humble nature of these wafers is something to meditate upon. . . . I urge you to try this experiment now: Let this book, *Inner Communion*, take the place of the white wafer. The book you are now holding in your hands is the Living Body of Christ. To take the Christ Nature which is Alive within this book and to absorb it into your Life—this is Communion. Invocation maximizes the efficiency of this Divine Process.

Now let us give our spiritual attention to this experiment: Breathe deeply for a few minutes; create a heart-centered energy of radiant thanksgiving and peace through this breathing: visualize this sphere of generated divine qualities expanding with every breath cycle to permeate the immediate area surrounding you to a distance of at least 10 feet in every direction. You have now created a resonating field that is naturally attractive to the creative intelligence of the universe. Continue to breathe and to hold this creative intelligence of the universe. Continue to breathe and to hold this meditation. . . . To awaken and activate the Spirit of Truth is the next step: Add the additional outward heart-radiation of Divine Praise to your generating sphere. The Fiery Quality of Praise always has a very special effect—the Shekinah, or Visible Manifestation of the Divine, is nurtured and illuminated by such a baptism of Praise. The final step before actual Invocation is now to be accomplished. Verbally and silently, affirm and pray with heart and will united in this effort—with energy, belief, thought and word, praise the Living Spirit of Truth. Send forth this radiant Praise to the Holy Spirit of Truth for several minutes, until you feel a Creative Connection has been established. It is essential to offer this Praise to Truth for two main reasons: (1) We need to give Divine Blessings before we can receive; (2) As stated above, Praise brings out the Shekinah or Visible Nature of the Spirit of Truth, so that all the spiritual senses may have something tangible to work with during and after Invocation.

We are now ready to consecrate this book, *Inner Communion*, by Invoking The Living Spirit of Truth. The best invocations are always created in the Here and Now. I will not offer you a written invocation here— it's best to make up your own. When the Will is clear about the purpose of the prayer or invocation, then the Words flow with ease from the Heart. Our purpose in this experiment is simple and clear: We are to invoke the Living Spirit of Truth to fill this book with Divine and Creative Blessings so that our Communion with it shall be of the Highest Use. We seek to establish a Spiritual Relationship with this book so that its Christ Nature may flow into our Body Temple and Aliveness in a totally efficient, fertile, and unrestricted manner. We seek to establish a "superconductivity" of Divine Relationship so that the Total Truth may encounter no resistance as it Joyfully Recreates our individual unique expressions of the Divine.

It is important to develop your own style of Invocation. Here is one classic style: When ready, raise your hands, with palms upwards, to the heavens. Verbally make your Invocation to the Holy Spirit of Truth. Inhale the Holy Spirit into your hands, and then bring this energy down into the center of your heart. Let the Holy Spirit unite with the Blessings of your Heart for an instant. Then exhale the combined Grace of the Holy Spirit and your own Heart out through your hands and directly into this book. If appropriate, the verbal Invocation may extend over both the inhalation and exhalation phases of this process. There are several variations involved here which you will discover through experimentation.

Now that our book-wafer is consecrated, it's time to feast! Enjoy these offerings gathered by Sondra over the last few years. Sondra Ray has deeply experienced Inner Communion with the Divine in a wide variety of situations, relationships, and sacred locations. May the moving and magickal potency felt at a transformational level by Sondra during the events she encounters on her Quest for Communion be shared with you joyfully through the consecrated medium of this book! Take your time and enjoy.... If you come across a thought or passage contained herein that particularly interests you, then pause and breathe, meditate, invoke, commune, explore.... The Waters of Infinite Life may burst forth from any and every situation.

In this new Aquarian Aeon of the Immortal Child which we are now entering, the *Liberation* of Communion is destined to develop as a principal description of the global and individual changes we shall experience. In old ways of thinking, communion is something reserved for special times and is only available from an intermediary priest. This Piscean Age attempt to limit certain times and certain situations goes against the very nature of the Christ Life which *Is* True Communion. The Christ Nature within each of us is forever proclaiming: "I am the Way of Everlasting Life! I am the Way of

Life Triumphant, Beautiful and True!" The Kingdom of Infinite Life is within You. Share this infinite Kingdom with the creator and the creation through every thought, word and action. In this Way, you fulfill your role in the Aquarian Liberation of Communion. Easter Everywhere and Christmas Everywhen—the Birth of Christ and the Triumph of Christ through the Immortal Transformation of Matter: These two events are perpetual and are happening totally all the time and in every situation. Mastery of the Art of Communion makes this Truth evident and opens the Way for you to become a Co-creator involved in both the Birth and the Triumph of Immortality at all times. In the Judaic-Christian Tradition, the True Masters of Communion are known as the High Priests and High Priestesses of Melchizedek.

Melchizedek is one of the most ancient Immortals mentioned in the Bible. One esoteric tradition suggests that he attained his Physical Immortality at the age of 52, after developing a perfect Angelic Communion with the Archangel Michael. Michael is the angel of Trust, Intuition, Sharing, and all forms of Communication—all ideal qualities inherent within the dynamics of Inner Communion. Michael is associated with the planet Mercury and Tree of Life sphere Hod. Fifty-two is one of the great sacred numbers: It is 4 x 13. Thirteen is the number of feminine unity: 52 extends this Shekinah quality to the four directions. Fifty-two is the number of years in one Heaven cycle in the sacred Aztec Calendar. We entered such a 52-year cycle at sunrise on 17th August, 1987 (Mexican time). This event was well publicized and was popularly known as "Harmonic Convergence." In the Hindu Tradition, there are said to be 52 different interpretations of the Veda and 52 corresponding pronunciations of "Aumgn (Om)" to go with each interpretation.

From the beginning, Melchizedek has always been devoted to the creation of the New Jerusalem, or the Earthly Paradise. This devotion of Will was clearly formulated during his Immortal Initiation through Michael. The present Work of the Melchizedek Priesthood is developing in harmony with the 12-year cycle of Jupiter. The present cycle began in 1987 and culminates in 1999. The primary goal of this period is to begin the activation of 52 Cardinal Sacred Sites on the planet. This work is to be accomplished in 4 cycles of 13 sites each over the next 80 years. As these sites open, they are destined to become places where the outpouring of the Grail Communion from Gaia intensifies to a state of superabundance and rapidly transforms the entirety of the planetary culture. At the times during the last few years when Sondra and I have come together at a site to do work together, our spiritual efforts have always been directly related to the advancement of this Melchizedek Work. Additional information on the 52 sites is contained in my book *Spheres of Destiny—The Shaftesbury Prophecy*.

The archetype of the Grail has always been at the heart of the Melchizedek Communion. As many of you know, the Grail Cup is far older than Christianity. It was used during the Atlantean Era by Enoch. It was used by Melchizedek to Bless Abraham and thus initiate the Jewish Spiritual Current. The Cup of Manna is one of the key forces within the Ark of the Covenant. Traces of the ancient Atlantean-Enochian Cup can be contacted through the Celtic myths of Ireland and Wales. The Cup which gives everlasting Life is found in many different religions.

The Arthurian Quest for the Holy Grail is the Quest for Perfect Communion. There is a Grail lineage and there is a Grail Communion. The lineage consists of all members of the Melchizedek Priesthood. The Grail Communion literally delivers what the outer churches symbolically offer—Christed Translation of the Physical Body Temple, or Physical Immortality. In alchemy, the Philosopher's Stone is identical to the Grail. The Elixir of Life and the Fountain of Eternal Youth are additional synonyms. The Christing of all Flesh is an inevitable result produced by Total Communion. This Christing of the Flesh is a Planetary and Individual process—hence the absolute importance as we approach the 21st Century to establish a deep and creative relationship with the Immortal Will of Gaia, the Living Earth.

When a New Revelation manifests upon earth, all the old Ideals which are asleep awaken and rally to the Eternal Cause. The Return of Arthur and Merlin as potent and creative forces at the present time are prime examples of this. We seek the Communion which transforms the Universe—this is always the High Way of Fruitful Travel.... All experience upon this Way offers the Infinite Magick of Immortal, Christing Communion....

Every experience offers Immortal Communion—yet how often do we completely accept and integrate at every level of being this Divine Offering? This New Aquarian Aeon is destined to be a cycle in time when humanity finally discovers *how* to accept and integrate this Communion. We all have a constant and ever-changing opportunity to partake of this Communion. Every instant of your experience is unique and shall never be repeated again. Each such instant of Living is offering you the Holy Grail. Certain mystics have always recognized this Truth. Now, in this New Aeon, all beings shall become Masters of the Spiritual Laws which interweave the Way of this Communion. These Laws are very simple to state and can be practiced in any, and every, situation.

At the present time, the space and time dynamics of the planetary Heart are expanding. This expansion of Gaia's Heart is creating a situation where suddenly, in the 1990s, there is more spiritual space in which to move. Relationships that have been stuck in positions of rigidity are now finding that new movements, and thus new relationships, are possible. The Immortal Anna Lee Skarin has stated that more men and women shall emerge as High Priests and High Priestesses of Melchizedek during the next 30 to 40 years than ever before in the history of the planet. This is due to the expansion of the Gaian Heart which we are now experiencing.

Paul, in the 8th chapter of *Romans*, has a profound Vision which describes the planetary Heart-Change which we are now in the midst of. He feels that all of creation is in the throes of Childbirth, waiting for the birth of the many Immortal Sons and Daughters of the Divine. For when these beings appear, then the entire universe shall be certain of Liberty—for the work of these Children of the Divine is to uplift all matter into frequencies above entropy, decay, and death. Paul was way ahead of his time in seeing the essential relationship between Gaia and individuals. The Heart-Womb of Gaia expands—and the Immortal Children of Global Regeneration emerge.

Rene Guenon, in his book *The Lord of the World*, offers many valuable insights into the Melchizedek lineage. The name itself is originally spelled Melki-Tsedeq, which means the Tsaddik of Malkuth. In English, this is translated as the Just Adept of the Earth. The Tsaddik is one who has *adjusted* his or her Being to a point of perfect harmony while Living on the Earth. In the Hassidic tradition, there are always 36 Tsaddiks on the earth at all times. When the process of Tiqqun, or material ascension, is complete, then Messiah appears as the 37th Tsaddik.

These 36 Tsaddiks are Perfect Heart-Masters, are physically Immortal, and are thus forever able to offer the Communion of the Grail. I would like to explain *why* there are traditionally 36 and to show their connections to the numbers 37 and 666. We often hear of 666 being the number of the Solar Logos and the ideal length of Glastonbury Abbey. These associations are all derived from the Hebrew Cabala.

In the Cabalistic Tree of Life, spheres are traditionally numbered from the Crown Chakra-Kether downwards. The Heart chakra-Tiphareth is numbered 6 in this pattern. Each sphere has a magical square. The square for Tiphareth-sun-Heart chakra is constructed by using its number 6: A square with 6 columns and 6 rows, or 6 x 6 = 36 sub-squares. Then the numbers 1 through 36 are placed in these 36 boxes so that each row or column adds up to 111. Thus the total value of the square of the sun is 666—the Solar Logos. Six hundred sixty-six is 18 times 37. Thus the 36 Tsaddiks maintain the planetary grid which grounds the solar-666 force which is Christing Gaia. In Cabala, the term which describes the work of the Tsaddiks, *Tiqqun,* also has the value 666. Tiqqun means the translation of all matter into Union with the Immortal Frequencies of the Divine—this brings us back to our theme of Communion. For True Communion always has as its Divine Purpose the Total Transformation of Matter in a Way that Glorifies Aliveness, Liberty, Light & Love. This is forever the Work of the Heart Master.

Each of the 36 Tsaddik Heart Masters is responsible for giving Immortal Grail Communion to 4000 individuals. This is how the number 144,000 is generated out of the Heart, for 36 x 4000 = 144,000. This number has been associated with the planetary changes initiated by Harmonic Convergence in August of 1987. To fulfill the prophecy of Analee Skarin, we are now in the process of creating over a hundredfold increase in Immortals on the earth.

At the present time the original 36 Heart Masters are focused in 12 groups of 3, each triune group acting as midwife at each of the 12 primary Gates of the New Jerusalem—12 specific sacred sites which are giving birth to the New Aeon. One Child is emerging from 12 wombs.... When this 12-womb birth is manifested and rooted, then the 36 Tsaddiks shift locations so that there is one Tsaddik at each of 36 distinct sacred sites. Within the next 30 to 40 years each Tsaddik shall have initiated a minimum of 4000 individuals into Mastery of the Way of Everlasting Life—Physical Immortality. The 144,000 are all now alive, incarnate. Sondra's Work in the Andes described in this book, *Inner Communion*, was specifically dedicated to Blessing the Birth of these 144,000. It should be noted that this number is a minimum figure—I am sure that many more than this shall find the Way of Immortal Communion before we advance to the midpoint of the 21st Century.

The above information on Melchizedek and the Tsaddiks is important. These ideas may be new to many readers. This is to be expected—for whenever we enter a new Aeon, in this case the Aquarian, the archetypes, spiritual laws, and ways of thinking change. The sleeping truths of old traditions awaken and join forces with the Activities of the New. Before leaving this contemplation of Melchizedek, I would like to illuminate our Theme a little further in one area. . . .

It is said of every Melchizedek High Priestess or High Priest that they are not born of earthly father and mother. This needs to be clearly explained according to the esoteric Judaic-Christian understanding of this idea. All of us, including Melchizedek, Enoch, Jesus, etc., are first born through the water-womb, with earthly mother and father. As we deepen our Mastery of Total Communion, we eventually reach the point of second birth. This preparation for the Birth of Fire may take many lifetimes or it may only take a few years. When we are *Re-birthed*, or *Born Again*, the Divine Within recreates us anew so that the entirety of our lineage or inheritance comes directly straight from the Divine. At this point we are born without earthly mother or father—not before. This second birth, where we are Born Again, is always identical to the Translation of Flesh—Physical Immortality. This has always been the goal of the contemporary Rebirthing Movement: The attainment of Christed Physical Immortality within the present incarnation. Never put off to a future Lifetime what can be attained in your present Life! All the Wisdom and Spiritual Techniques are available so that anyone who dedicates their Self to the Way of Everlasting Life can achieve Victory over all limitations—including the limitations created by the rejection of the physical body by the spirit. The marriage of Body and Spirit into a Living Unity in Service to God has always been the Highest Ideal of Divine Will within each of us. "Know ye not that your Body is the Living Temple of the Immortal Divine?"

The Way of Inner Communion leads to Perfection of what is known as "the Practice of the Presence of God." The ecstatic embrace of the Divine in each and every experience of Living is the Fruit of this Practice. Or as Sondra, in this book, quotes Heart-Master Da Love-Ananda as saying: "Love God to the Point of Absolute *Distraction*." Let me elaborate upon this idea of complete Distraction. Through the Way of the continually increasing the Heart radiation of the transformative qualities of Divine Praise, Love, and Joyous Thanksgiving, the visible presence of God becomes more manifest to all senses until *only* God is present. The totality of our spiritual senses unite with God in a tantric embrace which never ends at this point. This is Loving God to the point of Absolute Distraction. This is the state of True Communion. Total Communion always occurs at the point of Touch. In the Words of *The Invocation of the Omega Point*, "Oh Let my Touch be the Highest Manifestation for the Will Divine!

The Communion of the Holy Grail is always transmitted through the interface of Touch which is at the borderline between Self and God which vanishes during the ecstatic embrace described above. Consecrate and dedicate your senses to transmitting and receiving the Immortal Frequencies of the Divine totally through each and every experience of Living. It matters not whether your experiences appear to be either positive or negative—*all* experience is offering you the Communion of the Holy Grail. The embrace of all experience by the Radiant Heart of Joyous Thanksgiving unlocks the deepest Secret of Living here on earth and illuminates every Step upon your Way to Perpetual and Ecstatic Unity with the Divine. "Ye who are Grateful in All Things: Your bodies shall be filled with Light; and ye shall witness the Universe of Infinite Life outpouring from the Fountains of your Hearts!"

Sondra's experiences in Yugoslavia recounted in this book are very interesting. The Virgin Mary is one of the most famous physically Immortal High Priestesses within the Order of Melchizedek. She has been appearing in many locations over the last 150 years. It is important to understand the Immortal Nature of Mary. She did not die. She consciously translated her physical Body into an ascended Immortal Body. I have a strong Vision of her Dancing a Sacred Dance in Praise of the Divine at the Sacred Instant of her Bodily Translation. Three locations claim to be the site of this event: Ephesus, Jerusalem, and Glastonbury. We here at Glastonbury, the planetary heart Chakra, like to see her dancing in the area of the Chalice Well Gardens at the instant of her Translation.

For far too long, the traditional Christian Churches of the world have obscured the Way of Physical Immortality which Jesus teaches. This Way has been mastered by adepts from many cultures and religions. There are many Chinese Taoists who are Immortal like Jesus and Mary. There are many Immortals within the lineage of Black Hat Tibetan Buddhism. This Aquarium Aeon shall quickly witness a shift of focus from death to life— from the illusion of the crucifixion to the Truth of the Triumph of Life. Jesus was Physically Immortal *prior* to his crucifixion. Now is the Aeon to Regenerate the Universe through *Living*. In this Aquarian Aeon, death redeems *no sins whatsoever*: The Immortal Waters of the Holy Grail poured forth through the Living Heart *redeem everything*. The Water-bearer of Aquarius regenerates the earth. It is a profound Blessing to be Alive at this time upon the planet—for it is only through Living and Loving that the Will of Gaia is Fulfilled. May we each contribute our own Divine Unique Gifts to this Birth of a New Aeon!

True Communion produces a change within the physical body. When Moses communed with the Divine upon Mt. Sinai, his physical body became so charged with the Light of Truth that others could not directly look at him for a considerable time. When the Physically Immortal beings, Moses and Elijah, communed with Jesus atop Mt. Tabor (The Transfiguration), the Bodily radiance of all three was, again, too much for mortals to behold. When we blow our breath upon kindling to ignite and brighten a fire, we are following the same pattern to be found in Communion. In any direct encounter with the Immortal Divine, we have entered into a relationship which allows the Breath of the Divine to blow through our physical body at a sub-atomic level. Our Body could not become a Blazing Star in such a communion unless there was already alight spiritual kindling within every atom of our Flesh. We all have this spiritual kindling alight—it is called *Life*.

Mastery of the Art of Communion becomes possible when we learn the Way of making this Immortal Bodily Radiance perpetual. When the Breath of the Divine flows through the Flesh, the Light of Life becomes brighter. This Inner Illumination of the Body Temple reveals aspects of Divine Wisdom that previously were in darkness. The Divine Laws in Action during such communion become clear to consciousness.

We are all Christs in disguise searching for Ways of dropping the disguise. We are constantly trying to get the formulas right: How much should I give of myself in this situation? How much am I willing to receive? What do I have to give? To whom? Our minds generally do us very little good in this game. All too often, the mind, for an endless variety of reasons, places limitations to our giving and receiving of True Communion. I know of *no* Immortal who attained his or her Immortality through devotion to the mind. Ancient disciplines such as Zen are very valuable because they help us to create a state of No-mind. It is profound Initiation, especially for a left-brain intellectual, to discover that one is *not* identical to one's thoughts. Thoughts *can be* creative if we realize that thoughts are the servants of the Divine. In the West, we often say "I think, therefore I Am." In the East, we often say the opposite, "I cease to think, and thus experience my True Self."

Communion creates New Life. If we want to reconcile the above East-West polarity regarding thought, we need to unite with the forces which create thoughts. Every form of Communion involves Relationship: At least two Divine points-of-view agree to create an exchange of energy and information. To give New Life into a Thought, the two aspects which must agree to Communion with each other are *Will* and *Love*. Love is the Law—Love united with Will. Heart chakra united with Crown chakra; Tiphareth with Kether; Glastonbury (planetary Heart center) with Mt. Kailas (planetary Crown center)—in every situation, the Wedding of Love and Will is at the Foundation of True Communion. The Will to Love creates a Divine Relationship which makes Communion possible. True Love is the exchange of Immortal Divinity and always produces Joy. If you are breathing in the Fullness of my Christ Nature and I am breathing in the Fullness of your Christ Nature, then we are experiencing the Joy of True Communion. True Love is experiencing and sharing Immortality with a Point-of-view other than your own. Intellectuals who are attached to the "my thoughts are me" illusion find True Love very difficult.

In far too many traditions, the physical body and matter have been relegated to the bottom of the totem pole. The spirit, abstract ideals and archetypes, the intellect—all these things have been seen as somehow more Divine than the material. At best, the material has been seen as a passive substance which may be sculpted or shaped by the supposedly higher forces of the spirit and the intellect. In this New Aeon, this attitude is changing. The material is Alive, Intelligent, Divine, Creative. . . .

The Divine is meaningful only when it is perceived and experienced. Without the material, the experience of the Divine is impossible. "The Body is the Temple of the Spirit." As is evident in such great Cathedrals as Chartres, the Temple is capable of creatively using Spirit so that Spirit becomes meaningful, useful and beautiful. Rather than Spirit spiritualizing matter, it is matter which is materializing spirit. The New Age concept of our material earth as Gaia, the Living Planet with a Creative Will of her own, is another sign that respect for the material is increasing. The physical body is more intelligent than the mind, the cells of the body are more intelligent than the physical body, the atoms are more intelligent than the cells, and the iota particles (smallest possible unit of existence) have the greatest Creative Will and Intelligence of All.

If we go within and listen to the Wisdom of our iota particles, we drink of the highest and most profound Communion, for "the Kingdom of Heaven is Within You." Every iota particle is a bi-polar unity which is Immortal and offering the Communion of Love. When we communicate with this Level and honor this Will devoted totally to Immortal Love, then we begin to recreate our Being—this is often called "bringing forth the Christ within." Physical Immortality is the complete manifestation of the Iota Will. Let thy Will be done on Earth as it is in Heaven—Let thy Will be established without as it is already established within.

When we are born, the Divine gives us a Body Temple. It is the purpose of Life to translate this Divine Gift of the Body into Living Sacrament, and then to share forever this Immortal Life with the entirety of the Universe until all Creation is upraised to joyous frequencies of Liberty and Love. To be in the Presence of the Holy Grail is to be in the presence of a being who is Physically Immortal, or Christed. The resonating energy field of such a Grail Master radically transforms the immediate environment. The Immortal Will within the iota level of the surrounding environment—rocks, trees, animals, you—naturally responds to this Resonance of the Grail—inner and outer Immortal Will, the same in essence, unite to roll away the stone . . . to Liberate Christed Life.

In ancient China, the yoga of total Communion is known as the Way of the Tao. This Tao is best defined as the *ever-changing Perfection of the Now*. At every instant of our journey, there exists a way of relating to our experience which joyously maintains our ecstatic embrace of the Divine. As we advance upon our Mastery of the Way, our understanding of its dynamics changes from the complex to the simple. Whether the adept is Shinto, Taoist, Christian or Jew; the simple Fruit of the Quest almost always ends up the same in formulation: Embrace your experience of Living in the Here and Now with absolute joyous Thanksgiving. The total of all additional Wisdom and Theology is devoted to explaining *why* and *how* to attain this Divine Embrace . . . Through Faith and Action, the *why* and *how*—which are eternally inscribed upon your Heart—become obvious and precious. May the Everlasting Waters of the Holy Grail Grace and Bless thy Journey Forever and Ever!

The Communion of the Holy Grail may only be received *in* the physical body. Contrary to old Aeon ways of thought, death decreases Liberty. The separation of the spirit from the Body Temple at death is not in harmony with the highest Ideal of Divine Will and Plan. At death, the spirit sinks into a darker level of spiritual reality where illusion limits choice. As Stanley Spears says, death is a grave mistake. All humans who die eventually find their Ways back into the Physical Body until the Christing of Flesh through Immortal Communion is attained. It is only through Life and its Living that All things may be overcome. The Triumph of Life is the Highest Purpose of the Grail Communion. When the false duality between body and mind vanishes, then True Living begins. As the English poet, William Blake, realized, the Body and Spirit are One, not Two—they are literally the same thing. This alchemical Wedding is the constant and joyous experience of every Immortal, from Enoch to Mary to Analee Skarin. . . . And now the Immortal Christing of Gaia, the Living Earth, is beginning to manifest. We are Now Alive within the Birth-Joy of the Planetary Christ.

As stated above, this Planetary Christ-Child is emerging initially from 12 Wombs of Gaia—12 specific sacred centers. When Sondra was guided to light 12 candles in a cave in the Andes (described in this book), I intuit the Truth that she was creating a ritual to Bless these 12 Womb-Sites and the Immortal Planetary Life which is Now Being Born. May the Blessings of Immortal Birth be upon You and All Beings forever and ever!

The Power of Immortal Communion is infinite. Each and every experience of Living may be Transformed into Divine nourishment. Events which may appear to be vile, poisonous, or filled with sin can be

Changed into the Wine of Grace. The practice of Mary's 5-point program given at Medjugorje—faith, Dedication to the Divine, prayer, fasting, and peace—accelerates one's Mastery of the Art of Communion. I could easily write a lengthy book on the relationship between Immortal Communion and these 5 essential aspects of the Way. Perhaps at a later date. . . . To those of you who receive Divine Nourishment and Inspiration from your Communing with this book, I make this suggestion: After finishing this book, go within your Body Temple, invoke the Holy Spirit of Truth, and write 5 one-page meditations relating Communion to each of Mary's Keys listed above. If you get some good results, I would love to see what you come up with!

Inner Communion with the Divine develops when we learn to Trust the Word Alive within the Heart—and to Act upon what we Hear. This is Intuition. Sondra Ray is a woman who Trusts her Divine Intuition & Acts. She is a woman the Divine can "do business" with. Love and Will are shaping a Living Word within your Heart . . . Go within . . . Commune . . . The Divine has something unique and precious to Share with you Now. Together—in the Spirit of Sharing—may we spread our Fruits of Communion upon the Round Table of the World in Celebration of the Triumph of Life Abundant and Everlasting. . . . May your experience of Sondra Ray's *Inner Communion* contribute to this Feast!

—ROBERT COON
Glastonbury, England:
The Heart Chakra of Gaia
Pentacost, 1989

PART I

WHAT IS COMMUNION?

Easter Sunday, 1987

As a child in Sunday School, I was drilled over and over again on why our church denomination was the *only* church that was right about Communion. Some churches (which were named) believed that the wafers and wine were only "symbols" for the body and blood of Christ. Those churches, I was told, were obviously wrong. Other churches claimed that the wafers and the wine "turned into" the body and blood of Christ on the altar during the ceremony done by the Priest. Those churches were also obviously wrong. But, *our* church, which had the real truth (they said), taught that the wafers and wine became the body and blood of Christ only *after* they were taken into the body. We were clearly the only church that had it right; and since the sacrament of communion was considered nearly the most important thing of all in religion, we were somehow the "best" religion.

There was something about this whole thing that bothered me; but nevertheless I got an A on all the tests in Confirmation class. However, at my very first communion, I was so emotional about the whole thing that when the minister gave me the cup, I began to shake. I shook so much that my teeth knocked the rim of the

27

chalice and a loud ringing sound clamored through the whole congregation! I was so embarrassed that I was afraid I had ruined the whole ceremony.

Could it really be that religious fights actually occurred over this moment, this issue? I just did not like the idea that we were the only ones right and everyone else was wrong. It seemed like *separation*, not communion. Isn't communion, after all, the act of becoming one with all? Was it right to think I was becoming one with Jesus and yet separate from others? Did this make sense?

And later when my sister married, she did marry someone within the faith. However, since it was a different "branch" of our religion, I was not allowed to take communion in that church. That really got to me. Now there was more separation.

I wondered about this whole thing called Communion. Confession and Communion. It all felt very, very deep to me; and I used to really worry about those who did not do it. Does that mean they were not saved? How could they help it if they had parents of a different faith? Was I supposed to convert everyone to my faith? I had so many questions and got so few answers. (What about those in the third world countries? Are they saved?) I felt guilty if I did not take communion, and if I *did*, I felt guilty for being "special" for being better than others. It just did not come out right.

I felt we should be "communing" with all our brothers all over the world, not making ourselves separate. If one is truly communing in love, can he place himself superior to any brother?

How does one be in "communion" with all of our brothers and sisters of humanity? How does one be in communion with all of nature? How does one be in communion with higher beings? How does one be in communion with one's own higher self? Or with Life Itself?

I like very much what Sir George Trevelyan said in his Foreword to the book by David Spangler, *Revelation: The Birth of a New Age*:

> The great seers and adepts of our age have shown that it is possible to reunite with the *Primal Oneness* which, in a condition of absolute being, life and creative thought, underlies all the created world. This amounts to a true form of conscious exploration into further dimensions. It involves indeed a blending of consciousness in heightened awareness with beings from higher planes. This is the new and true COMMUNION for our age, which carries us beyond the trance medianship which characterized the earlier generations of spiritualism. A VERITABLE NEW RENAISSANCE COULD COME IF THIS MENTAL COMMUNION WERE TRULY ACHIEVED. There is nothing that could not be done....

In church it seemed like we needed the sacrament of "communion" to have forgiveness and absolution; and it seemed like we had to take something from outside of ourselves, something separate from us, and put it in ourselves to get communion. But what if our consciousness *was* blended with the Primal Oneness and with higher beings at all times? What if this great knowledge and love came from within ourselves? We could then solve the immense problems facing us today. Sir George acknowledges David Spangler as one of those kinds of beings who has developed this power.... He says David is coming from this kind of blending when he speaks and writes. (This becomes obvious as you read his book.) He *is* an inspiration to all of us. He has what I am calling "Inner Communion."

This is, of course, our goal in Rebirthing . . . and the goal to be obtained by using all of the spiritual purification techniques I have mentioned in my earlier books, such as *Pure Joy*. A few souls, like David Spangler, came in with this blending highly developed and were able to maintain it. We all have this potential, but many of us were sidetracked and thrown off center by our birth trauma and other karma we had to complete. Thus, purification is necessary to get one back to that inner communion, which is, I believe, a natural state, without ego.

David himself describes being conscious of two worlds: the normal world revealed through the five senses, and the metaphysical world of light, energy and essence . . . home of intelligences more evolved than our own. He says that that dimension can be reached through intuition, meditation, ESP, and states of altered consciousness. For David, the Universal Presence from the higher plane identified itself as "Limitless Love & Truth."

Although I had met David briefly after he completed his work at Findhorn, I did not read his book at that time, nor did I even see it. It was only after I was guided to write *Inner Communion* that his book was placed in my hands by a member of my own staff. I then realized that David represented the very state that I wanted to write about. If I do nothing more than convince people to study the works of David Spangler, I would be very satisfied that I had accomplished something major. Who he is and what he is saying is that important. However, the goal of this book is for all of us to realize that potential within ourselves, that potential to experience constant communion and live in everlasting peace. . . .

I thank David for reminding us that communion is based on *identity*. If we are going to transmit messages from higher intelligences or if we want to commune with beings like Jesus, we must *identify* with those beings, and with those qualities communicated. We must integrate and become that and be that; and it must be ongoing. . . .

Communion and Happiness

*I*nner Communion is experiencing the state of supreme happiness or Pure Bliss. People are always searching for happiness and bliss and this comes from not understanding the truth. The truth is that your very reality IS happiness and bliss. Unhappiness is something we make up and superimpose on our natural state. Therefore, if you are unhappy, it is up to you to find out what it is that you are doing to your natural state of happiness. In other words, misery is something we give to ourselves. It is up to us to discover and release those thoughts that we have used to distort our basic happiness. All of my books have been about this, in a way, and all the methods of spiritual purification that are mentioned (esp. in my book *Pure Joy*) are ways to rediscover your happiness by purifying yourself of anything you have used to cover over your happiness. These methods do not make you become happy, they clear you of thoughts that keep you from being happy. If you think that your unhappiness is real, this is a mistake in your thinking. God is real. God is bliss. You are one with God. Only the ego attempts to distort this reality. But since the ego is not real, and is only a collection of negative limiting thoughts based on the false premise, "I

Am Separate," which is not real, then those negative thoughts that arose out of the false belief of separation are not real either. We are constantly trying to make imperfect what is perfect and then blaming others for our unhappiness and imperfections.

Inner Communion is being aware of what IS and being aligned with that all the time; and not losing sight of the fact that that IS one's very center, one's core. It is ALWAYS there. IT does not go away. Communing with Divine Spirit is always possible; but we must first wake up to the fact that we have not been utilizing this potential. We have been turning away from the light or Spirit, by covering it up with our ego.

There is an article I read by Heart-Master Da Love-Ananda called "The Transmission of Happiness."[1] He describes the process of awakening to Spiritual Communion like that of learning to use an organ that most of us don't even know we have. He says that what must take place is more than just changing your mind, more than inner awakening, more than having a good feeling about everything. There must be, besides those things, a literal change of the whole body in order to be enlightened. There must be changes in the nervous system, changes in the body chemistry and functioning of the brain.

How does this come about for a person? There are purification processes such as rebirthing and chanting as mentioned in my book *Pure Joy*. Traditionally, the appearance of a Master is highly valued for this reason: masters are able to transmit and magnify the presence of Spirit in another by their mere presence and or writings. I can honestly say that by submitting myself to these Beings I have received a glimpse of full potential. As a child, I had the example of Jesus. As an adult I was blessed by the presence of several Eastern adepts including Saibaba, Muktananda, and especially my master Babaji. Recently I have placed myself in the presence of The Virgin Mary in Yugoslavia and The Divine Mother in India. I have immersed myself in the energy of the Holy Spirit through *A Course in Miracles* and I have studied some of the works of Da Free John. I honor with great devotion these beings who have purified me and given me this transmission or "current." However, if I had not first learned to understand myself, I could not have received it to the extent that I have. As I continue to receive it, I can continue to transmit it to others. Heart Master Da Love Ananda says it this way:

> When you have contacted the Spirit most profoundly, then you can live your whole life with the spirit and give yourself up to it altogether.[2]

Devotion and ceremonies of ritual worship are ways of tuning into the energy of Spirit. Anyone who goes to the Islands of the Gods (Bali) can see the whole population performing pujas (ceremonies of ritual worship) daily. Everyone does this naturally before starting the day's work. The results are astonishing. In the six weeks I spent there, I saw virtually no fear, anger, or conflict. The Balinese people were not only angelic, they had perfect bodies. I saw no one who was overweight. Everyone seemed to be radiating that Inner Communion.

Spending time in India, one is amazed to discover that all they really care about is how to be more devotional. I have seen hard core "cases" (resistant, negative, blocked, closed-down people) go through a sudden melting and opening of the heart (displayed by sincere weeping) when they were given the opportunity to participate in devotional communion with the Divine by Chanting. I have seen many major transformations in people who achieved Inner Communion by choosing to be in constant service to the Divine in their work and external life.

So, I ask you, what are *you* doing about this? If you are not currently doing spiritual practices on your own, perhaps you need the support of a group that does.

Again, I would like to quote the Heart-Master Da Love-Ananda:

> There is only one process that makes a difference, the process of distraction in God. That is what the practice of spiritual life is. *It is the only thing that is worth doing.* Everything else is a hellish evolution of desires and complications of form. There is only one way to be saved, and that is to love God to the point of absolute distraction.[3]

Christmas Day on a Boat in New Zealand

Christmas is a time for celebrating joy, of celebrating peace, and of celebrating Christ Consciousness. Being in Communion with Christ on this day is the whole point, but what *is* the Christ? *A Course in Miracles* explains that Christ is the "Perfect Son of God" or "Christ is God's Son as He created Him. Jesus became identified with Christ; however, it was a mistake to think that He was the only one who could be Christ. Is He the Christ? Oh yes, along with you."[4] Jesus became what all of us must become. He led the way for us to follow Him.

Jesus also saw the face of Christ in all his brothers and remembered God. In other words, He did not see His brothers separate from God either. He saw them as one with God just as he saw Himself. He did not make the separation real; He did not make what was false true. He came to save us from the illusions that we have made up; and He continues to function in this role. He remains with us to take us out of the Hell we made. (The *Course* describes Hell as being what the ego has made of the present, or what we have made out of the present with our egos.) Walking with Jesus, who is completely in Communion with the Christ, is like walking with a brother who has completed his part perfectly. We are wise to follow Him and unwise not to.

But how can we follow Him when we may be left confused and hurt by our religious upbringing, which may have felt controlling and unsatisfying in the results that we saw? It is obvious that we did not get what He was saying two thousand years ago. If we had, we would not be suffering. It has been said that the presence of Jesus on the planet was so pure that it has taken two thousand years to process the amount of ego that came up to be purged! Now Jesus is giving us another chance. He has come again in modern times and in this New Age through *A Course in Miracles*. He explains everything and answers everything. It is a clear way we can follow Him and be led from the hell we made to Heaven Consciousness. The *Course* is one of the best ways I know of to establish Inner Communion. It is not a religion. It is not a path. It is a correction.

You may complain that your life does not work, but are you willing to do what it takes to make it work? The *Course* is actually a required course because we all eventually need to learn its message in order to be saved. If we don't learn it from these particular books, we will have to learn it another way at some point, which might take longer.

The *Course* says that for Christmas we should give the Holy Spirit everything that would hurt us. The Holy Spirit is the Voice for God, the remaining communication link between God and His separated Sons. The Holy Spirit gives us the answer to the separation, which is the Atonement. The Holy Spirit abides in the part of your mind that is part of the Christ Mind. Jesus is the manifestation of the Holy Spirit. You are also His manifestation in the world. Jesus is one of the helpers we have been given to enable us to remember that we were also created in the image of God, just like Him. Jesus is the bearer of Christ's message: the love of God.

We must not let despair enter our minds this Christmas, or on any day. We can be in joy NOW because we are deprived of nothing, once we remember who we are. We need not sacrifice anything. Our communication with Christ remains, whether there is a body or not. . . . communication is not of the body, it is of the mind, which is never sacrificed. Jesus proved that in the crucifixion and resurrection.[5]

I must add that if you still feel entrenched in the idea that God is separate from you, then what is said here will not make any sense. The *Course* itself is designed to unravel that untruth in your mind. I suggest you read it and re-read it until you are liberated from that lie. The truth will change your life forever. To make it easier to understand *A Course in Miracles*, I have created a workbook called *Drinking the Divine*.

Communion and Physical Immortality

On Christmas Day I always try to listen to Handel's "The Messiah." Did you know that this miraculous piece of music actually teaches the knowledge of Physical Immortality? How many of us were ever taught the true meaning of the words? I have covered this explanation in my book on Physical Immortality, *How to be Chic, Fabulous and Live Forever.*

For the purposes of this book, I would not feel complete without mentioning the fact that to me Inner Communion includes being so at one with the life force that even death (the last enemy) can be overcome. In case this is the only book of mine you have read, I will include a short summary of the topic here, hopefully to whet your appetite for further study.

Are you aware that the body was designed to be able to live thousands of years?

Are you aware that several people mentioned in the Bible lived over 5,000 years? (How did they do that? If *they* can, *you* can.)

Are you aware that there are immortal masters who can dematerialize and rematerialize at will, and that they are around and available today? In the Bible Melchizedek was one. Jesus, of course, is one. In modern times, we have the examples of Analee Skarin, St. Germain, Babaji and others.

Are you aware that you can actually meet people who are hundreds of years old? It is very common in India. (I met one woman who was 400 years old.)

How do they do this?

They are obviously in total COMMUNION WITH THE DIVINE, WHICH IS ETERNAL.

> There is an answer.... The knowledge of mastery of Physical Immortality can be yours. The power of Physical Immortality can transform the earth into paradise. It can completely transform your body. Your body can be renewed, regenerated, immortalized. You can learn to dematerialize it and rematerialize it. The adepts are willing to teach this information.

> There are available spiritual purification techniques to help us master the spiritual laws necessary to be physically immortal. The truth about this can transform your whole body, your relationships, your entire life ... and the quality of life on the planet. You can have pure joy and live as long as you choose.[6]

Understanding the possibility of Physical Immortality must begin with the certainty of spiritual enlightenment. That includes certainty of the truth that your thoughts produce your results, or that thought is creative. Negative thoughts produce negative results and positive thoughts produce positive results. *A Course in Miracles* teaches that "Death is the result of the thought called the Ego, just as surely as life is the result of the thought called God." The ego is a collection of limited negative thoughts we have formed that keep us from re-membering we are one with God. The main thought of the ego that we use to kill ourselves is the thought that "Death Is Inevitable." This thought, like any other lim-iting thought that we made up, can be changed. It can be breathed out of our consciousness. We do not have to go into agreement with this thought just because our ances-tors did. If we change all of our thoughts that make us age and die, and use spiritual purification techniques (such as Rebirthing), we can get different results.

The most important thing is to remember the truth: we are one with God, one with the Spirit, which cannot be destroyed. If we think we are separate, then of course we think we lose our connection to the vitality of the Source. Jesus also said in the Bible: "The power of life and death are in the tongue." By this He meant that what you say is what you get with your body. Very few peo-ple in the past were ready to master Physical Immortal-ity, but some did—Jesus, Babaji, St. Germain, Enoch, Melchizedek, Analee Skarin, for example. There have been many more that can be studied. These immortal masters are willing to teach us now. The world is ready to hear this information now. There are many books being written on the subject. Here are some: *Beyond Moral Boundaries*, by Analee Skarin; *The Life & Teach-ing of the Masters of the Far East*, by Baird Spalding; *The Door of Everything*, by Ruby Nelson; *Rebirthing in the New Age*, by Leonard Orr & Sondra Ray; *13 Steps to Immortality*, by Robert Coon; *The Book of the Holy Grail*, by Robert Coon; and *Physical Immortality*, by Leonard Orr.

Some people will say "I would not want to live forever because I want to go to a higher place." And yet, you do not necessarily go to a higher place just because you drop your body. Consciousness, when departing from the body, seeks its own level. There is no escape from yourself. Death is no solution. Other people say, "I don't want to live forever because it is too painful." The reason it is painful for them to be in their body is because of the death urge. Therefore, mastering Physical Immortality IS the solution to manifesting a body free of pain. This is the "Catch 22" ... the secret of the ages.

People who are sick obviously do not want to live forever, and yet mastering Physical Immortality is the way to heal sickness. In fact, all healing is temporary until you heal death. We could teach people to heal themselves of all the diseases they created (because what you create you can uncreate), BUT if they don't heal death, they will just make up a new way to kill themselves. It becomes clear that all death is suicide.

There is an alternative to aging and death and that is youthing and mastering the mind and body so that you can keep it as long as you like by the power of your mind. If you can learn to rejuvenate your body and youth it (which you can) and if you can learn to live in a body free of pain (which you can) and if you can learn to have and maintain Pure Joy (which you can), then you might want to learn to master Physical Immortality. The quality of your life would immediately improve.

ROBERT COON

As many of you know, Robert Coon, my Immortalist colleague, consultant, and friend from Glastonbury, England, has been very generous in sharing some of his writings with me. From time to time he allows me to publish bits and pieces in my latest books, for which I am very very grateful.

The pages I have written here (with his permission) are from his book: *The Revelation of Physical Immortality*, on which he is working.

I picked out some of my favorite paragraphs from his manuscript which give me the feeling of intense joy. . . . Thank you, Robert Coon![7]

"In this New Aeon we are witnessing the spiritual Liberation of matter. In the old age we were wrongly taught that Liberty is obtained by escaping FROM matter. Contained within the Heart of all matter is the True Will for Everlasting Life. When this Will is expressed, then matter and Will are liberated."

"To find Peace, the entire being must be sanctified, or freed from the influence of sin and death. The fusion of body and spirit into service to Life gives Peace. Death is warfare between matter and spirit. Immortal Life is Peace forever due to the wedding of matter and spirit. To pray for Peace on Earth is to pray for the Christing of all Flesh."

"'Blessed are the peacemakers: for they shall be called the children of God' (Matthew 5:9). The children of God are those who have made this peace between matter and Spirit and have been born again. Lasting Peace can only be established through the Work of Physically Immortal beings. When we complete the process of rebirth, we acknowledge the totality of our inheritance as coming directly from the Divine. The Immortal Nature of God is completely transmitted to each of us at the moment of rebirth or transfiguration. The Transfiguration is that moment when your Physical Immortality is established. Jesus attained his second birth atop Mt. Tabor when he conversed with the Immortals Elijah and Moses."

"We begin with thought. Every thought should be filled to overflowing with the Will for Everlasting Life and dedicated to the overcoming of all mortal boundaries. Be an alchemist of thought—give joyous and immaculate life to every creation. That which is created immaculate is free from the corruption of death and decay. Abandon all deathist philosophies."

"Enthusiasm is essential. Immortal enthusiasm is generated from constant *COMMUNION* with the Divine at the deepest atomic level. Enthusiasm means to be filled with God . . . ravishment of spirit . . . divine motion. . . . Every great Prophecy is revealed to the prophet during a state of deep enthusiasm."

"The vessel of the Grail is the Physical Body. Gratitude is the most expansive spiritual quality. Immortal Flesh continually radiates thanksgiving from every atom and cell of the Body. To be in the presence of the Grail is to be in the physical presence of a Physically Immortal human being. To seek the Holy Grail is to seek Physical Immortality."

SERVICE, WORSHIP AND RITUAL

To be in a state of communion, one must realize what one's duty is in being here so that one is not endlessly "flailing about". It has been said that one's purpose is self-mastery and also to be a "caretaker of the planet." My Master Sri Babaji always taught us that we are custodians here on Earth and that we have a duty: we must assist all life forms to a state of greater development and well-being. Service to others is our main duty.

Through "karma yoga" we help mankind to return to the natural order of things. We are to choose activities that keep us focused on Divine Truth. He taught us that "Work is Worship" and all of one's work should be dedicated to God.

We also need rituals as a center of focus for the mind. Worship is extremely valuable as a way of purifying the heart. We must glorify all forms of life. It is our duty. We were taught to use sound, light and fire. We practice the mantra Om Namaha Shivaya, which Babaji said is the highest thought in the universe. It contains all the five elements and it is the ultimate sound. There is great power in chanting the mantra. It is Infinite Spirit, Infinite Being and Infinite Manifestation. We use light in ceremonies to meditate on Babaji's external nature, the formless nature where there is nothing but light. This reminds us too that the visualized form is a being of light. We put grains in the fire and feed it back to the Source, honoring our abundance and at the same time we symbolically burn our karma. By doing these rituals we re-energize the life cycle by re-directing the energy that has been bestowed on us.

These rituals of worship are explained very completely by Shastriji, Babaji's high priest, in my book *Pure Joy*.

PART II

COMMUNION IN SACRED PLACES

Machu Picchu, Peru

A very special time to "commune" with the spiritual masters is during the Shamballic Wesak Festival. When you connect with the masters, you are connecting with a wondrous power; and it is a good idea to find out when their festival is each year because it varies with the astrology. Fredric Lehrman and I scheduled a spiritual retreat during this time at the incredible lost city of the Incas: Machu Picchu, Peru. This Inca sanctuary is the site of temples and palaces which were built around 1420; it is located about 8,000 feet above sea level in the most inaccessible part of the grand canyon of Urubamba. The city was such a well kept secret, that for three hundred years it was unknown. Only Inca nobles, priests and priestesses and the novitiates, or Chosen Women of the Sun, were permitted into the sacred precincts of the sanctuary. The character and the mystery of its construction surpasses most marvels imaginable. Although its true function is unknown, there is much evidence to indicate that it was designed for religious purposes, constructed as a convent and special palace for these special women called "Virgins of the Sun," who were chosen from the empire's nobility for their talents and physical perfection.

This incredible white granite city was ignored until 1911 when Hiram Bingham, an American teacher with a strong interest in South American history, discovered it. (It was covered with vines at the time.) It is now a popular tourist center. Fredric Lehrman and I had long been aware of it as a major power spot with very deep sacred significance. So we began this pilgrimage with approximately 78 students accompanying us.

Before leaving, we had received important papers from our fellow Immortalist, Robert Coon in Glastonbury, proposing that we try a global activation technique involving a large map he had sent with the major earth chakras and energy flows outlined. He reminded us that Machu Picchu is the global sexual chakra and listed recommended activities for each day of our trip. We were given important prayers, meditations and invocations all leading up to May 13, 12:50 GMT, when the Wesak Festival culminated. He explained to us that the Immortal Masters would be giving a harmonious outpouring of New Birth and Blessings to the earth during the days of the Festival and we were given certain ceremonies to do to help release to the world whatever Love, Praise and Gratitude, Joy and Light we would be building up during those eleven days. We would link up our global acupuncture with a group of conscious Immortalists in Glastonbury and be in communion with them.

After making it through a total power block-out in Lima (terrorists had bombed the power station), we were relieved to be in Cuzco, where we stayed for two days to adjust to the altitude. We began our devotions, chanting, prayers and *A Course in Miracles* studies in order to open up to the Masters and the energies. The night before we arrived at Machu Picchu itself, we made it as far as a hostel near "Aguas Calientes." Here we decided to purify ourselves even further by wet rebirthing everyone in the hot springs at sunrise the morning of the departure.

The evening meeting before that group rebirth is one I shall never forget. One of Our Loving Relationships Training graduates from Florida, Kathy, a Unity Minister, stood up in class and said she had the worst headache she had ever experienced in her life. Her head was splitting in two, she said; but she was also seeing an *amethyst* in her third eye. I told her to lie down immediately in the back and begin nasal breathing ... I knew she was about to have contact with something or someone. I proceeded to teach the group, attempting to read from a most exciting new manuscript *Rebirthing the Earth*, by Robert Coon. Robert had lent me a chapter called "The Priesthood of the Order of Melchezidek," and he had asked me to write a preface to this book and I was very thrilled. This chapter was so interesting that the class was hanging on every word: but the more Kathy breathed in the back, the more tuned in I got to what was happening with her and I could not read well. Suddenly I was hit by a very powerful energy moving in a block toward my heart chakra. I stumbled over the words. Pretty soon I could not pronounce anything, not even the simplest words. I told the class I was going to have to lie down in the back and rebirth myself. Fred took over. Don and Lynn, who are body workers, came over and helped Kathy and me. We breathed and breathed together and at one point, Kathy had quite a surprise.

Babaji appeared to her in a vision. He was wearing a poncho (which I thought was cute). He showed her Machu Picchu from above and pointed out to her a room she was to take me to. We were to do a ceremony and take twelve candles with us. We had no idea where this place was; but I assumed Kathy would recognize it when she saw it.

The next morning at sunrise, we all climbed the hills with our snorkels in hand and went to the hot springs, where we got in, en masse, and rebirthed each other in twos. It was quite astonishing to breathe in hot water at that altitude! It was one of the deepest purifying wet re-births I have ever been a part of. And then we were off to the Lost City of the Incas, which was a lot harder to get to than I even imagined. We had told the class to go in in silence, find a spot they each individually related to and do a private ceremony of their own choosing. (Fortunately we were allowed in after the tourists left, which is one of the reasons we had such a powerful experience.) I have never been to such a powerful place other than Babaji's ashram in the foothills of the Himalayas. I wondered if the tourists really got what was going on there . . . they seemed to run in and run out, chatting all the time, not listening. We stayed three days and we spent most of that in silence and ceremony.

The first night I followed Kathy's instincts, hoping she would recognize the spot Babaji had showed her. The only problem was that most of these ancient ruins had no roofs, and she said the place he showed her had a roof. "Do you suppose it is a cave?" she whispered to me. I found myself agreeing, saying that would be Babaji's style. Then I asked our sweet guide if there were any caves around there. He said, "There are lots of caves."

"Take me to the best one," I pleaded.

"You are very near it," he whispered. Kathy's intuition had been good. The entrance, however, was so subtle and unlike a cave entrance, that we would have never found it, had not Babaji showed it ahead of time. We marvelled at the beauty of it and set about the twelve lit candles. There was Fred and me, Kathy (who had the vision), and Don and Lynn, who had helped Kathy and me during our rebirths. We all meditated for about twenty minutes but then we had to leave as it was getting dark and the guide said everyone had to be out of the ruins by a certain time. I was told to come back on my own.

The next day most of the group wanted to climb Mt. Huayna Picchu, but apparently they were not ready. There was a storm and a lot of people got sick. Obviously, we were supposed to calm down and get adjusted. It was very clear to me that everyone was getting a major purification, including myself. At 3:00 a.m. I awoke to find there was a fire on my altar. I vomited and then I said, "Thank you, Babaji." I had experienced these fire purifications before, and I was grateful I could go through it quickly. The third day everyone felt quite different and most of the group climbed Huayna Picchu. I went back to the cave.

In the cave I was able to experience the communion I was looking for. I took Don with me in case I needed my body adjusted. I also felt he was going to receive some information. We stayed quite a long time and I found it to be a very, very graceful experience. Fortunately, I had taken a bit of paper and I jotted down what information came to me in meditation. I "saw" a rejuvenation center actually; and I was given lovely names of different temples that are to be inside. It was so beautiful and so graceful that I cannot adequately describe the feeling. In this cave, I was also instructed to go alone to Medjugorje, Yugoslavia (right after Harmonic Convergence) where the Virgin is appearing.

Later when I was relating this to some of the people who had climbed the mountain, one told me that she had seen Babaji floating over the cave we had been in.

Another ceremony that we did as group was at the site of "Death Rock." It is a huge rock shaped into the form of an altar. It is a block of one piece with three steps. While the whole group chanted, we each took turns lying on it, surrendering ourselves as much as possible to the death of the ego. Actually it was quite like an instant rebirth. One could feel there had been powerful rites performed there.

Nobody was disappointed by our experience at Macchu Pichu. In fact, each of us gained, personally, a lot more than we expected. It was our goal to move ahead to Lake Titicaca, where we hoped to be at the culmination of the Wesak Festival. Due to a train ride that took eleven hours instead of the expected five, we were a little behind. But one of the other big highlights for me was visiting the Island of the Sun, right smack in the middle of Lake Titicaca, which is the highest lake in the world. We were only allowed on this island for thirty minutes, which seemed unfair after such a long boat ride! We begged for more time, explaining that we had important ceremonies to do. We finally were given an extra half hour. So we climbed the big hill and began the ceremony . . . only to be interrupted by the guards shouting that we had to leave immediately. The boat was leaving! We tried to explain to the guard that we had been given an extra half hour but he did not believe it. The group panicked and began running down the hill. Fred and I and Kevin finished the ceremony as we felt it was of major importance. The boat came back for us and when we finally took off, we complained that we had been interrupted. Then we asked if they would mind turning around and going back to shore so we could do it over without interruption. We were determined to do it correctly. Now I will share with you the Invocation we did to open the channels for the world to accept Physical Immortality:

LAKE TITICACA

I call upon the Spiritual Presence
  Of every Being of Love and Truth
  To Hear and Heed this Invocation!

Oh may the Spiritual Guardians of the Andes—
  And every sacred site—
  Be nourished and sustained with the Fruits
  Of Everlasting Life!

From the Waters of Lake Titicaca,
  I call upon the Immortal Flame of Viracocha*
  To Arise! Arise! Lord of Life!

Great Creator of All Life,
  Bless this Union of male and female,
  Of Sun and Moon!
  Oh Bless this Union

Of the Two Great Feathered Serpents
Who embrace our world with Love!

Oh Let the Perfect Children
Of this Marriage NOW come forth
From every Heart upon this Planet—
With Joy, with Light, and with the Spirit of Liberty—
To establish forever and ever,
A Paradise of Immortal Beauty and Everlasting Peace!

And Now—
In total harmony with the Spirit of Truth—
May All Immortal Masters from every Tradition
UNITE
To send forth the Highest Divine Blessings
Of Joyous Gratitude and Loving Light
To heal, to awaken and to vitalize our Mother Earth!
May the Living Flame of Viracocha Illuminate
The True Will for Immortality throughout this Universe!
There is Now an Answer! Let it Be! Oh Let It Be!

*Viracocha: In the ancient tradition of the Incas, Viracocha first appeared upon this earth as the original creator by rising up out of the waters of Lake Titicaca. Then Viracocha created the sun and the moon, male and female, and all things yin and yang upon the earth. And now in this New Age, Viracocha rises up again to bless the union of male and female and the Immortal Children of all such unions. As the sustainer of all Life, Viracocha traditionally possesses the Divine Quality of Luminous Eternal Youth. Incans who lived to an advanced age attributed their longevity to Viracocha. The Aztec Quetzalcoatl and the Mayan Kukulcan are equivalents.

—Information for the Wesak Full Moon, 13th May, 1987.
Key time: from noon to 12:50 p.m. GMT.

Harmonic Convergence

On August 16 and 17, 1987, people of all ages and backgrounds quietly went on pilgrimages to sacred sites. What we were all doing was praying for peace and welcoming in the New Millennium, which had been marked on ancient calendars as a major turning point. To me it was not just some "hippie event," as it was made out to be by part of the press and media. The fact that people all over the world did get together and commune in this way in such great numbers, shows a new acceptance of the New Age consciousness movement. (It *is* working its way through the culture and *is* being taken more seriously.) This network of people is optimistic and willing to honor spiritual laws ... they want to make the world a better place. An event like the Harmonic Convergence helps transfer mass consciousness to a higher level, which obviously has to happen to reverse the tendencies of going toward destruction. I was, of course, also interested in the fact that everything was supposedly shifting to the "Feminine Ray." This would balance things out and was something to celebrate. I chose Glastonbury as the sacred site for me, for several reasons. It has been called the current "Heart Chakra"; my friend Robert Coon, our great Immortalist colleague and consultant lives there; and besides, I received a message the year before in India that that is where I was to be. Later, Fredric Lehrman and I were invited to speak with Robert in the Town Hall.

Yes, there were all kinds of people there: visionaries, seers, sages, healers, punks, other immortalists, old ladies and so on. But we also had Sir George Trevalyan, the "spiritual father" of Europe, and Rupert Sheldrake, an amazing holistic scientist who talked about the planet being ALIVE, not some dead mineral as science once thought. The whole point of these days was how can we live in such a way as to serve a LIVING planet? And that is where we came in, with Physical Immortality.

It was one of the greatest privileges of my life to be on the stage with my two immortalist colleagues, Fredric Lehrman and Robert Coon. We were sold out in the local Town Hall. There was standing room only. Since Frederic and I usually teach this as an advanced class for LRT graduates, we are always curious how people "right off the street" will accept it. Not only was our lecture totally accepted, but the questions we were asked were sincere and conscious, showing an eagerness to learn the information rather than reflecting any kind of cynicism. In fact, we were, after four hours, given a rousing, standing ovation.

Later people begged for more, and those that could not get in the Town Hall insisted that I offer another lecture for them. This time I used to answer questions; and I was willing to talk about any one of the subjects that I teach around the world. Everyone seemed to want to know about Babaji, and the excitement of tuning into him was having a phenomenal effect on my second audience. People wanted to know about the Immortal Masters, and they wanted to feel my vitality as much as possible and they seemed to know how to draw it out of me. Even the people in town who ran the shops and could not attend the lectures were being affected. In fact, my last conversation in Glastonbury went like this: I was in the bookstore buying some cards. I went to the cash register to pay and the clerk suddenly blurted out: "INSTANT IMMORTALITY!" I was very surprised and so was she. Then she added, "I don't know why I said that . . . " She had not attended my lectures and did not know who I was!

What does all this have to do with Inner Communion? A lot. If you will study our books and lectures on Immortality, it will make total sense. But for now, I can put it this way: being in true communion with the Divine is naturally regenerative. If you live constantly in God communion, via spiritual practices that are life supporting (such as purification with breathing, etc.), longevity is a natural by-product.

Being in total communion with the all-pervading Life Force IS the Fountain of Youth. This Universal Life Energy is willing to continue to sustain your body indefinitely, unless you think otherwise.

SUMMARY

The Harmonic Convergence was a world inter-dependence celebration.

It was also called "The International Sacred Sites Festival." It was an internationally co-ordinated, multiple-location event. Recruitment went on for a group of

144,000 who took part in synchronized twelve-day purification ceremonies culminating in shared dawn rituals held over a forty-eight hour period. The common theme was Healing Planet Earth and Peace among her people.

This signaled a phase shift in planetary evolution which marked the passage from a collective perspective of CONFLICT to one of COOPERATION. The success of it was due to a remarkable grassroots world link-up.

These individuals, linked together through resonant attunement, formed a kind of Human Battery. This helped shift the collective mental field, which is our beliefs, shaped by collective memory patterns that make the world as we know it today. Rupert Sheldrake calls this "field" of human experiences the "morphogenetic field." Creating a new morphogenetic field is the way to change the world. This can be done by a "trigger event" to shift the collective mental field. It was the end of an old mind set and the beginning of a new one.

Follow-up events: this event was the beginning of many that follow. Some people even planned thirteen events from Wesak of 1987 to Easter of 1990. These highlight three years of spiritual work to fulfill prophesies of peace.

The Miracle at Medjugorje, Yugoslavia

In August 1987, I was "called" to Yugoslavia, where the Virgin Mary had been appearing. I don't recall when I first heard about this miraculous event, perhaps it was a year before I actually went. When you hear about it, it is the sort of thing that "stays in your mind." I did not immediately decide to go, because Yugoslavia seemed like a remote Communist country, and I was much too busy. But then one day in 1987 while meditating in the cave in Machu Picchu, Peru, I was clearly being told to go. It was a strong message that came into my head. I did not hesitate, as I learned long ago to follow my strong messages. I did not wonder if it was real either; somehow I was personally convinced that the apparitions were authentic, even before I went there (even though I am not Catholic). Now I found it interesting that it never occurred to me that I was not Catholic or that I knew little or nothing about the Virgin Mary. It never even occurred to me that there would be thousands of Catholics there. I just went; and I went alone.

I viewed the whole thing as something very important, regardless of religious affiliation.

Apparently, the apparitions of the Virgin Mary began on the Feast of John the Baptist, June 24, 1981. The Blessed Mary began to appear to six young people who live in a little hamlet called Medjugorje, which is located in the remote inland mountains and hills. Mary has continued appearing daily since 1981; and although the young people are usually the only ones who see her, millions have flocked to this little village, many coming in prayer groups. The Lady of the apparitions has identified herself as the mother of Jesus and has asked that the young people refer to her as the Queen of Peace. They see her every single evening around 6:30 to 6:45.

Perhaps the most important thing is: Why? and What is the message? The principal message can be put into one word: PEACE. And this, according to Mary, has to do with "Right Relationship to God." Because of our rebellion against God, things are falling apart at the seams; society is breaking down, wars are multiplying, violence and terrorism are increasing, family life is suffering greatly and on and on and on. All this disorder is affecting nature, and we are also bringing upon ourselves more natural disasters. Mary is warning us that if we continue on this path, we will be facing even worse consequences. We are neglecting God's ways; Mary says it is our sin that causes the evil we suffer.

Mary states that without a large-scale turning to God, very, very dark days are ahead. A political solution will not work, she says. We will not have peace until enough people turn away from sin. She urgently stresses CONVERSION and proposes a five-point program:

* Commitment to God
* Faith

* Prayer
* Fasting
* Peace

She says that when humankind is at peace with God, only then will it truly be at Peace. She says that the power we need comes from the Holy Spirit.

Mary's role is that of a Prophetess. In this role, she speaks for God. She says that if enough people get back on the right track, the coming catastrophes can at least be mitigated to some considerable degree. (The purpose of prophesies IS to change them.) This message in Medjugorje, however, is a *serious* warning to our world which has been in the process of destroying itself.

About one week after I decided to go to Yugoslavia, someone in the U.S. handed me the following paper, which does summarize some of the history. I don't know who wrote this and I can't seem to remember who gave it to me. There are apparently many newsletters like this one being circulated around many different countries.

VISIONS OF HEAVEN

Thousands of lives have been affected by reports of the appearance of the Blessed Mother in the small village of Medjugorje in Yugoslavia. These reported apparitions have taken place almost every night for more than two years. In 1983, over 300,000 pilgrims traveled to the town on June 25, the date the Madonna of the apparition has requested be set aside as a new feast day honoring Our Lady "Queen of Peace."

Six teen-age children (two boys and four girls—ages 10 to 17) have witnessed the appearances of the Blessed

Mother. The apparitions began on June 24, 1981, on a mountaintop behind the village. The children claim they have received daily visitations since that time.

When the apparitions began, there were numerous reports of miraculous events similar to those at Lourdes and Fatima. The news of cures and miracles quickly spread throughout the region causing increased devotion and a deepening of faith. People began traveling to the site on the mountain where many have testified to the visible signs of mystical phenomena. In August 1981, the people saw the sun begin to spin and move towards them as the earth began to darken. On another occasion a fire blazed between the earth and heaven on the mountain. When police raced up, they could find no sign of burning. In addition to this, all saw the word "MIR" (PEACE) written across the evening sky in letters of light.

On other occasions during the actual visitations, a brilliant light appeared around a huge stone cross erected on the mountain peak. This cross is said to have been seen spinning in rainbows of light almost every day.

It did not take long for civil authorities to intervene in the events. Officials of the Communist country were alarmed with the vast numbers of young and old openly demonstrating their faith.

One of the first steps taken by the government was the arrangement of special activities and dances to attract the young people away from their prayer rituals. However, the youths ignored the alternatives and demonstrated a preference for prayer, sacrifice, the eucharist and Bible studies.

The next move was to curtail pilgrims by cutting off transportation, blockading roadways, and preventing cars from entering the area. Yet crowds continued to flock to the site on foot through rugged mountain terrain.

Realizing they could not stop the devotion, government officials fenced off the mountain with barbed wire. Anyone venturing beyond was promptly arrested. The local police then gave orders to the pastor that no religious assemblies could take place outside the church. Since that time, the apparitions and prayer meetings have been taking place inside the parish church.

Shortly after the mountain was declared off limits, more repressive measures were taken against the parish priest, Father Joso Zovko. For failing to recant his witnessing of the miraculous events, he was sent to prison. In addition to this, the six visionaries were picked up by the police and severely threatened without success to force them to deny the apparitions. Yet, the children were not afraid and claimed that Mary was right there with them and the police could do with them what they wishes. The children were eventually released.

The teachings from Medjugorje are Christ-centered. The Blessed Mother described by the children encourages reconciliation and conversion among Christians and promises peace for those with faith. She begs for sacrifices, prayers, and repentance. She instructs us to read the Gospel and live in accordance with its message. She reminds us again, as she did at Fatima, to pray the rosary and to receive the sacraments.

In addition to this, the Blessed Mother has reportedly revealed a total of 10 secrets to the children. These secrets will be delivered to the Holy Father on a future date.

The Madonna has identified herself as the "Queen of Peace" and her message is one of peace for the world.

The children say that this is an inner peace brought on by personal conversion. The apparition has also told the visionaries that the world is on the brink of a major catastrophe caused by sin in the world. This catastrophe cannot be avoided but its days may be shortened. For this reason the Blessed Mother urges faith, daily prayer, monthly confession, sacrifice and fasting. At one point she said, "Christians have forgotten that they can stop war and even natural calamity with prayer and fasting."

The present pastor of the parish reports that serious sin has been virtually eliminated in the parish. The entire community fasts on bread and water every Friday, and the young people fast three days a week. In addition, they attend daily Mass, and visit the Blessed Sacrament frequently. On the average Sunday, 35 to 50 priests are needed to hear confessions between morning and evening Masses.

The children describe the Queen of Peace as wearing a brilliant white veil and grayish-white ankle length dress. She has a lock of curly black hair visible on the left side of her face. Her complexion is said to be typical of the country girls of the area, with rosy, olive-colored cheeks. Her head is surrounded by a brilliant crown of stars. She is usually smiling and her hands are lifted up from her side towards the heavens.

Although it is my personal view that this is an authentic miracle of our time, it is for each individual to determine and to decide what it means for him or her. Everyone has their own very personal experience at Medjugorje. I have decided to share my personal diary, *uncensored*, instead of writing up another kind of report, quite simply because I feel it is more poignant this way.

As I approached Medjugorje, my taxi driver reminded me that there are no hotels . . . that was about all the English he seemed to know; therefore, I felt it was useless to ask him what to do. I was on my own, on a prayer. Then I saw hundreds of people walking. And then hundreds more milling around. Because I had all my luggage, my driver took some pity on me and stopped at a few houses to ask if I could board there. Not a chance. Full.

I wondered what I would do; but I chose faith instead of worry. It worked. A little boy approached and pointed up the road. My driver put him in the car . . . how sweet he was! (How many times I have been helped in foreign countries by little boys who directed me. I recalled them all in gratitude!)

I was driven a few miles from the church into the village to the edge of a tiny town. When the family welcomed me, especially the grandfather, I burst into tears. No one spoke a word of English, but their warmth was astounding. I was so relieved to have a bed and a family.

Soon I made my way back down the hill to the church, where I was suddenly in church during Mass. I saw everyone crowding and trying to get into a small room on the right. I assumed it must be the room in which Mary had appeared before (now she apparently appeared in the Rectory). Naturally I tried to get in, but it was impossible. Later, however, as I calmed down, I was allowed to join an American group for a small service in English. This was a great blessing and the wonderful American priest was giving a talk on the meaning of Mary's prophesies. He clarified that they were not intended to create fear.

"Whatever happens is going to be good, but we must prepare," he said. The good will be for those who are ready spiritually. (However, if you are not ready, it could be horrible.) The end result, however, will be VICTORY. Hate will become love. Perversity will be changed to purity. Disunity will be changed to Peace, and Sin will be changed to the Wine of Grace."

He said that what Mary is saying is simply this: CONVERT NOW / PRACTICE FAITH / PRAYER / & FASTING. WE MUST CHANGE. He reminded us that "spiritual pain is worse than war" ... and that we had been chosen by "Our Lady" to hear this talk and we had been so honored to be in that room. Then he gave us all communion.

I walked among the hundreds of people and spoke to a few in the afternoon. Everyone seemed deeply religious and simple. I was impressed with the humility of everyone I met; and especially all the European "grandmothers" who were holding up in the heat remarkably well. I saw many crippled in wheel chairs, many children, and numerous "prayer groups" that had come. People were fascinated that I had come alone.

At 2:00 p.m. I was back in the church listening to a message by Father Z which was translated. He talked about the fact that Mary's main aim here was Peace: "Peace is the aim. Conversion is the way. Prayer, faith and fasting are the means." To convert means to find your way back to God. (It did not seem like he was saying convert to Catholicism. This whole thing seemed to be beyond any particular religion.) And then he talked about what was fundamental; the special presence of Mary at Medjugorje. She had at that time appeared for 2,300 consecutive days! She was saying she wanted to fill us with peace and joy and the love of God . . . but we must be open, he said. He warned us not to say, "I don't have time to pray," or, "I can't fast."

I was happy I was doing fine on the third day of my fast. It seemed right. He reminded us we can fast much more than we think we can. When we fast, a new space is created for God. Then we were reminded that if we pray, it will be easier to fast. If we fast, it will be easier to pray. I was in fact experiencing this and had experienced it many times before. Mary is recommending that we pray every single day and fast two times a week. This time she says it is imperative.

In the late afternoon, I decided to interview a few priests. I had hardly ever spoken to a priest my whole life, so this was a breakthrough for me. I found them very cooperative. I began with Father S, who was Yugoslavian but spoke perfect English due to his training in the States. (His American passport had been taken away from him by the authorities; this was my first real reminder I was in a Communist country.)

He proposed the study of just why do all the people come here? We should search for the secret power behind it all. His theory was that Mary is giving FRESH AIR to the world . . . and that people come here to have their deepest desires fulfilled. People have their emptiness filled here, he said. He told me that man has lost the sense of God as the CREATOR. God is intervening here to bring man back. He reminded me that Mary is speaking to every human being, not just Catholics. I asked him what Mary meant exactly, when she said CONVERT. He said it means "Become a good human being. . . . A good human being in terms of being in *Holy Communion with God and Man.*"

Then I told him I was writing this book, called *Inner Communion* . . . and I asked him to elaborate on communion. He suddenly went "very deep" and penetrated my soul. Here is what he said:

"In order to fulfill our purpose with meaning, man must be in Holy Communion with God and then man. Jesus said, 'Love God with all your heart and then love your neighbor as yourself.'" Then he drew a cross. "Holy Communion is not only going up the cross, man to God, but also across, man to man in communion." Something about the way he said that made me cry. Then he said, "I don't want to push you, but what is conversion to you?"

All I could say was, "It must be ongoing, right?"

"Ah yes," but his question has stayed with me.

ARE WE CONVERTING OURSELVES EVERY DAY?

At four o'clock people began crowding around the rectory hall, the place of the apparitions. The apparition occurs every day at 6:45. It was pretty clear to me that the sick would go in and the visiting priests; and I certainly did not try to push my way to the front, as it was clearly impossible. After several hours of Hail Mary's, the crowd gasped and began staring at the sun. I had heard about this miracle, but to see it directly is another thing. This occurred approximately 15 minutes before Mary came. The sun began spinning. It seemed to have a rose pink glow and one could stare at it directly with no problem. All I could say to myself was, "I have seen a miracle."

At 6:45 we all knelt down as the priest next to me said, "Mary is here." It was quite obvious that something awesome was going on inside that room. The next day when I awoke, I felt like a child. Many lines from my face were gone. I was greeted by a jovial Italian man in the room next to me who said (we communicated in Spanish) how surprised he was to find out I was so big. He said he thought a child was sleeping next door. . . .

SECOND DAY

The Italian couple invited me to go up on the mountain with them. They would drive me to the bottom of the hill, they said, and we could hike up together. It was on this hill, June 1981, that Mary first appeared to the children. We started out early to avoid the mid-day heat. My new Italian friend and his wife told me that Mary appears there in gold on every August 5, which she told the children is her birthday. There is a large cross at the first site on the hill, and then one up farther on top of the hill, where she moved to later. People tie their handkerchiefs to the cross and leave prayers. It is said that there will always be something special left at this site forever, even after the apparitions cease. As we came down, hundreds were climbing up, many actually carrying the sick, maimed and disabled. This stirred feelings in me that I hardly knew what to do with. And then at the end of the trail, a man collapsed. I could not tell if he was beginning the hike or ending it, but he suddenly latched on to me for dear life. He gripped me as if to take from me every ounce of vitality he could, then he had a seizure. He recovered, but I was a bit shaken; this was soon changed by crowds of people praying loudly who came between us.

In the afternoon, I became very quiet. The thing that seemed appropriate was to sit and wait and observe. Soon I was inspired to begin my regular devotions. I found an old chair and sat outside the rectory, which contains the current apparition room. Since I am not a Catholic, I just went ahead and did my own regular devotions: prayers and chanting. Chanting the Aarti felt right because, after all, it may have been Babaji who sent me here. And it felt good to merge the energy of the Mother with that of Babaji. (Besides, I *was* on my way to the Divine Mother Festival in India.) A man came and sat under the tree where I was chanting. It seemed he liked it very much . . . even though it was in Sanskrit. It was while chanting that I looked up and saw the girl who had translated the service into English yesterday. I went up and thanked her and told her I was writing a book. Then the Father came out and I explained to him that I was willing to relate any message to the world he would like. He said I could come at 5:00. He did not exactly say that I could come into the apparition room . . . and he was gone before there was time to ask. Did I dare to think that was what he meant?

I was not attached to having that happen. Of course, it would be a wonderful kind of miracle . . . to be able to actually go in. Everyone, all the thousands, naturally dreamed of it. I of course wanted to go in very much just like everyone, but I had faith that the right thing would happen, which might mean that it was more important for others to go in. I tried to remain unattached to the whole idea . . . yet I was also very willing to be a "reporter." Well, anyway, he did invite me to *something*.

So then, at 3:00 pm, I began my vigil. I sat near the steps of the rectory. Since I was the first one there, I got the one and only chair. It does not really matter who gets there first; people are not let in on that basis. The Virgin Mary and the Holy Spirit let the priest know, I was told. But I wanted to be early so I could see and so he could see me, just in case he did mean that I should go in. I already knew it was no guarantee you could get in even if you did get permission. Some ladies told me they had had permission, but they got so mobbed at the gate that they did not even make it. I tried a cooler approach, being seated, relaxed, wearing my bright orange prayer scarf on my head. The same priest had seen me in it in the morning. And yet, I did not feel dressed right for the occasion. I wanted to bathe and put on pure white; but no chance. I did not dare leave the area nor risk wearing something other than what he had seen me in earlier.

The mobs began at four as usual. People were handing up bags and bags of rosaries from the different groups, to be placed in the apparition room during her appearance. Everyone gathered around . . . there wasn't much breathing room at all. People were shoving and pushing at the gate. The guards, with turquoise bands, had to push them off. I sat quietly on the side of the railing about a third of the way up the steps. Then many old women came around and began saying Hail Mary's. At first I was a bit unconscious, but after hundreds of repetitions, I finally heard it: "HOLY MARY, MOTHER

OF GOD, PRAY FOR US SINNERS NOW AND AT THE HOUR OF OUR DEATH. AMEN." I did not like this programming for death going into my body. It was getting louder and louder and finally my shoulder developed an acute pain. I dared not leave my spot and there was no escape; I was "packed in." Finally, I turned my front to the side of the steps to give my shoulder a break and I began saying loudly "Hail Mary, Mother of God, pray for my innocence and physical immortality so that I may spread your word." This brought me considerable relief. Suddenly I saw the Franciscan priest gathering up those who had been chosen. It seemed like he had chosen all visiting priests. I understood this, as it was a Sunday. People began shoving and pushing. Then the priest called *me!* I tried to get through but there was NO SPACE TO MOVE. There was only one way: I leaped through the railing bars! The crowd gasped, thinking I was cheating. (I was glad I was thin enough to crawl through!) And then the priest led me up the rest of the stairs, so that the crowd realized I was "legitimate." I was, quite frankly, very surprised to be going in; after all, it was only my second day!

The room we entered was tiny . . . it seemed like a very simple library. We all crammed in. To my surprise, I was there with around twenty Catholic priests. The only other females were two camerawomen. We all stood and prayed for about a half hour before Maria came in. For some reason, today she was the only visionary present.

When she came in the room, a hush came over us all. More Hail Mary's. She kneeled down. I wanted to think the right thing, pray right, be right, get in the "right" state. I wanted to be totally humble like her. I wanted to surrender. I started sweating. Then the man in front of me became faint and left his spot. I was "pushed down" near the visionary named Maria . . . I was right between her and the priest! What Bliss and Glory to be near her. After all, the Virgin had appeared to her literally thousands of times.

There was another lengthy prayer preparation, led by Maria. Then the priest told us that the time was coming; and when Maria stopped praying out loud and went into silence, we were not to speak or film. When the apparition began, I looked at Maria's face. It was a rapture and ecstasy that I shall never forget. And the ecstasy in her being was totally natural! She was obviously captured by a supernatural phenomenon, something very, very mystical. Even though the rest of us did not "see" the apparition of Mary, a very intense thing took hold of us. I began to cry. We all cried! And then, I suddenly and spontaneously grabbed my uterus. It was a very feminine energy hitting me. . . . I was "spacing out."

And then it was over. (The apparitions used to last twenty to thirty minutes, but now they last only three to four minutes.)

I felt speechless. Something immense definitely did take place. . . . As we came out of the room and down the steps, the cameras were popping everywhere. People came up and touched me and there were many different comments in languages I did not understand. Some people even grabbed me, holding on. Some Canadians asked me how it was. "I am speechless," was about all I could manage. I went outside. The sun was still doing its spinning. Someone told me that the white part coming forward represented the Eucharist, the Host.

I saw a large peach aura around the big cross on the hill. It changes colors, they told me, and that cross has also been seen spinning. I wondered what that cross on the hill was about. . . . Someone said it represented the FAITH of the local people.

It seemed like thousands of people were flowing around the church. There was no room to get in. Along one wall of the church were priests available for confession in all languages. Lines and lines of people waiting. Someone came up and told me about all the miracle healings that had occurred, how her friend had been healed of cancer, and on and on. I was in a daze. I began walking back to my village.

THIRD DAY AT MEDJUGORJE
(Fifth day of fasting, also my birthday)

Today, on my birthday, I felt anything else gained after being in the apparition room would be pure gravy. I wanted to take it easy and get very relaxed and surrendered. I wanted to integrate. I began the day with the simple things like picking wild purple flowers for my altar. To my surprise, this brought me as much joy as being in the apparition room! Could it be that my holiness would now pervade everything? I took the hike to the church, walking slowly. As I approached, a woman came up to me saying, "I was so privileged to meet you right before you went in the apparition room. I saw you coming out. You put your prayer scarf over your head . . . you are the holy one." I did not really know how to reply to her and all I could do was see the holiness in her. I went into the English Mass. The priest was talking about how Jesus had done prayer and fasting in the wilderness to strengthen himself for public life. This is what I felt like I was doing.

The priest was reminding everyone that what we appreciated here was meant to change and transform our lives so that we will have total sincerity in our daily lives in order to inspire others. He warned us of the danger of going back to the routine daily life, the "soft life," he called it.

I spent the morning writing gratitude cards to my staff, over juice in a little tienda. An American woman approached me with her daughter. She was on her way to Lourdes. She had come to Europe for the healing of her daughter who she said had severe birth trauma. (She was "breech," and when they pulled her out her arm was caught around her head and there was severe nerve damage and lack of movement.) I found it so amazing she would approach me, after all my years of researching birth trauma and rebirthing. Since it was difficult for her daughter to walk long distances, it was quite hard to walk down the country roads and search for a room in the farm houses. I was able to help out since the Italians in my family house had just moved out. My heart bled a bit again for all those children damaged at birth. . . . I felt sure I was in the right profession.

(So on my birthday, I *received* the pleasure of giving in this way. It felt really good.)

The afternoon lecture in church was about the last public message (July 1987) given by Mary. She gives one per month, on the 25th of each month, and since a new one is expected tomorrow, the last one was reviewed. I copied it down: "Dear Children, I beseech you to take up the way of holiness, beginning today. I love you and therefore I want you to be holy. I do not want Satan to block you on that way. Dear Children [and here she means all people, not just those children she appears to], pray and accept all that God is offering on a way which is bitter. But at the same time, God will reveal every sweetness to whomever begins to go that way and he or she will gladly answer every call of God. Do not attribute importance to petty things. Long for Heaven. Thank you for your responses to my call."

The priest then gave a talk on the desire to be holy. Even though I still somewhat resisted the "Catholicness" of it all, I did get inspired to create a "Holiness Workshop." I certainly did agree with the idea of valuing holiness above all else.

I was feeling closer and closer to Our Lady, Queen of Peace. I was trying to understand what it was like to be a Catholic. I did not feel pressured by all the Catholics. I chose to go to Mass, since I had never done that in my life and since all activity was in the church. Then, I decided to go to a priest for confession. I had never experienced that. Maybe I should on my birthday.

I confessed to him that I was not a Catholic and that I had been offered communion and I took it. We had quite a lively discussion on communion: Protestant vs. Catholic. He told me not to do it again. Of course, that was no surprise; but I wanted to know why it was wrong. Then we had some real *debates*. He asked me about my spiritual practices. He told me breathing techniques were pagan. I just could not relate to that at all.

Changing the subject, I quizzed him on this thing Mary says when she tells people to convert. "Now she is not implying everyone should convert to Catholicism, is she?" I inquired. I was fairly wired up, convinced that he would imply that *anything* other than Catholicism might be pagan. However, it seemed since I was raised a Christian, I was okay, or "in the ballpark," but anything besides Christianity was pagan. I could not deal with that either. He really put down India. I tried to explain to him how Jesus had appeared to me in India and that any place could be spiritual. We got nowhere . . . it almost went from bad to worse. Then I was reminded how religious wars got started. Here we were, trying to honor Mary's plea for Peace, so I dropped it, seeing how easy it would have been to go deeper and deeper into our differences. I could have headed for a huge conflict, but I calmly went back to my question about the word "convert." (Somehow I had gotten myself into interviewing the priests about that.) He said, "You are bit uncomfortable kneeling this long, aren't you?" There were many in line to come to confession. I was obviously holding it all up . . . but he kept going on and on with me.

I do acknowledge him for giving me such a long deep answer about conversion. He quoted Jeremiah 33: "I will take away your heart of stone and give you a heart of flesh." He said, "A heart of stone is impervious to God; it is non-caring, stuck in darkness. The word of God cannot be united with a heart of stone. We must convert our hearts . . . this is an unconditional pre-requisite to God's activity. Conversion means turning away from sin. . . ." I did not want to get into a discussion with him about original sin. It was very tempting to bring up

A Course in Miracles but there was a long line and I was already "on the edge" with him. . . .

One sweet thing that happened on my birthday was that an Irish man came forth in church and sang a song which he had been inspired to write on his way to Yugoslavia. It shows, I think, the kind of deep feelings and love with which people approach this experience. His name was Finbarr Dynan, from Cork, Ireland.

MEDJUGORJE

From Cork's green vales we fly,
Going eastward through the sky,
Until we reach that stoney hill,
at Medjugorje.
Young people saw one day,
A Lady on the hill,
Our Queen of Peace just standing there,
at Medjugorje.

CHORUS: Avé, Avé, Avé, Our Queen of Peace we pray,
We will sing for you and pray to you, at Medjugorje.

Some said She was not there,
Yet the sun danced way on high
And then they saw her prayer for Peace,
Scrolled on the midnight sky.
Now thousands throng to pray,
And She visits every day,
Sometimes in bright blue and white
Sometimes she's clad in grey. (CHORUS)

"I am the Blessed Virgin,"
She said on that first day,
Do tell my daughters and my sons,

To fast, repent and pray.
Young people of the world,
Do not turn from Her away,
With anxious love She's calling you,
From Medjugorje. (CHORUS, twice)

It was quite delightful, in the Irish accent and tune. I approached him and asked him about the line "scrolled on the sky." Then he told me that in the beginning of the apparitions, there were many non-believers; so Mary wrote *MIR* (Peace) *in the sky*!!!

FOURTH DAY
(Sixth day of fasting)

Today in church the message was that whatever brought us here was a call from Mary. She wants us to be Crusaders, called by her Son. We are going to spread the message. We are instructed to be successful crusaders with fervor. We will find the strength. Our worries and ills will melt away because we were called and we answered the call. . . . We must respond with an open full heart. We must not say "I can't fast." No mother brings to her child a task that her child cannot achieve.

It seemed everyone in church was taking this quite seriously. I did also in my own way, but not interpreting it as a Catholic would, I am sure.

I wrote down all my prayers today, petitions to make my work much better and purifications I wanted in order to prepare for my true public life. I wished I could put them somewhere appropriate. Then the priest said right after that that he would collect any petitions written and take them into the apparition room. I had no idea anyone else was writing anything down.

Today we were shown a video on the history of all of this. It was a very well done documentary by the BBC. I was amazed to learn that over four and a half million people had visited here. It also said that these are the last appearances that Mary will ever make in the world. The political issues discussed around church and state were quite amazing. The video was very convincing, not that I needed any convincing. It was all pretty obvious to me: it was and *is* really happening.

In the afternoon, I sat outside the apparition room again, doing my devotions. The crowd was really riled up today since it is the 25th and another public message would be given. I was sitting around chatting with various Americans who had come over. Their religious devotion was remarkable. They began giving me sermons about the power of the Holy Spirit and quoted me Bible passages right and left. I must have been particularly good at listening today, as I attracted a lot of these "lectures."

Right before the apparitions began, an evangelist walked up to me and handed me her personal rosary. She said the Holy Spirit told her to give it to me and that I was going to receive the water of life and I would never thirst again. Then after the apparition she told me to walk with her through the fields. She was giving me so much of her heart, I went along. She gave me a real sermon walking through the vineyards, saying I would know when I found the real thing, which was Jesus Christ. I did not have the heart to tell any of these sincere people that I was very fulfilled with my religious life and that I had read *A Course in Miracles* four times and so and so on. I just let them all talk to me. I was very open and I tried not to judge when I felt they were trying to convert me to Catholicism.

Then the priest whom I had clashed with the day before approached and said he had been thinking of me. He handed me things to read about the rosary. I *wanted* to ask him if he was now willing to see that God was in India and everywhere; and would he also be willing to really hear that I had had the most converting religious experiences of my life in India; and would he be willing to hear me this time when I told him Jesus *did* appear to me in India? After all, was I not open to receiving a rosary and the books?

All of this went through my mind; but I decided to keep my mouth shut and start my relationship all over with him.

FIFTH DAY
(Seventh day of fasting)

I was much too serious today. I forgot to have fun. I started the morning okay with the cold water, but was rather irritated with the dirt in the bathroom. I made the long walk as usual from my farmhouse to the churchyard (three miles?) in a fairly holy space, finally noticing that they were doing one mass after another (in different languages). I was eager to hear the English mass to find out the public message from Mary the night before. It was straightforward enough. I was waiting for the priest to elaborate; but he said it, sat down, and that was it. I spent the morning feeling rather weird. Something was a bit strange in the upper part of my body. (Was it fear?) I was briefly tempted to stop fasting; but I did not really want to end the fast. After all I was not at all hungry. Why "stuff" this feeling with food? Why not go through it? Did I really expect to be here and not go through *something*? It was not so bad that I could not stand it, after all. It was no surprise that I also attracted weird situations.

A large man at the coffee house was complaining loudly how things were around here. He was actually sitting there writing a letter to the Pope, who he was intending to see on the Pope's coming visit to the U.S. He was very serious about his complaints to the Pope. He was reading his letter loud to a woman in his tour group and to a nun. He was protesting that this nun, whose name he mentioned in the letter, was shoved about after having waited three hours to get into the apparition room. He was also furious that a little boy had been knocked to the ground. He was reporting to the Pope that the Franciscan monks should be thrown out for doing a poor job in organizing the place; and did he, the Pope, realize people were going to be killed? The nun raised her voice loudly, "Take my name out of there . . . I don't want them coming down on me!" (They got in a big debate.)

Then he demanded to know: "Why are you afraid of Rome?" I got kind of "involved" in my mind, since I had nearly been trampled myself. I could, after all, teach them a very organized simple fair method I had learned in South India for handling masses of people who really wanted something all at the same time. I *saw* it work. Of course, "they" (Rome, the Catholic Church) would never listen, because after all, I learned this in India, and they think India is stupid and pagan. I started taking sides with this man. Finally I went to another spot to clear myself. I felt a bit weirder. I then remembered that I could use my own techniques on myself and I quite simply wrote down my feelings and thoughts on paper and cleared them. Some fear of my future role in the world; yes, just a few old thoughts lurking. I went into the church and did some long prayers by myself; and I finally got through it.

But everything still felt serious to me. Where was the fun, the excitement?

The sermons went on in church: We were asked to pray from the heart . . . were we merely praying from the lips using a multiplication of words? Are we saying we do not have time to pray? Did we realize that an average American family spends seven hours and ten minutes a day watching TV? And we dare say we don't have half an hour to pray in the morning and in the night? (Well, that was a fairly interesting thing to think about . . . I got mildly aroused.)

And the sermons went on and on: We are in the service of the message of Christ. Mary is entering our life and wants to stay with us. She wants to stay with us when we climb the hill of the cross ("She'd better," I thought, "I am, after all, going to tackle it tomorrow.") The purpose of her presence here is to make us realize she is with us. We should learn to live in her presence. We should become a Queen of Peace ourselves. We must stay in Holy Communion with God. How? Fasting/Prayer/Conversion. What is conversion? It is saying: "God, I am on your side." It means staying on God's side . . . that includes morality/honesty in life and business. I could not argue with any of it. ("Yes, but let's have some fun!" I would say to myself.) Every day they went over and over it.

I went out of Church and started over. I walked up to the man who was writing the Pope and talked to him. His group brought me coffee. They told me some things I found interesting to know. One woman at the table had bought hundreds of Medjugorje souvenirs to give to others so that it would be a seed . . . she said she was convinced if she gave an *object*, a more lasting impression would be made on the mind. I began to see how it all was working, the whole plan. Mother Mary was very smart. She was certainly getting everyone's attention.

In the afternoon, I found out her REALLY BIG PLANS. The evangelist came by again and grabbed me. She had been allowed to visit and interview Maria, the visionary girl I had been with during the apparition. Each visionary child was complete, she said, after they had been given ten secrets. She, Maria, was the last child, and she had been given nine. [This must mean that the showdown is close (I had really gotten here under the wire).] "And what happens *then*? Did you ask her?" I wanted to know.

"Oh, yes . . . then Mother Mary is going to manifest a huge sign over that mountain over there and the world will be shocked; and all doubt will be gone about her really having been here. The day before she does it, she will tell the children, they will tell the Priests, and the Priests will tell the world. They have," she added, "a direct line to the Pope."

"But, of course," I thought. "That would be logical."

I finally had a little watermelon (which I did not consider was cheating on my juice fast).

Mary's Message for the Public—August 25, 1987:

"Today also I am inviting you all so that each of you decides to live my messages. God has permitted me also in this year, which the Church has dedicated to me, to be able to speak to you and to be able to spur you on to holiness. Dear Children, seek from God the graces which He is giving you through me. I am ready to intercede with God for all that you seek so that your Holiness may be complete. Therefore, Dear Children, do not forget to seek, because God has permitted me to obtain graces for you. Thank you for your response to my call."

I was only able to gather up a few samples of the other messages that had been given. I was hoping to find a book where they were ALL written down in English; but the only thing I could find out was that the paper had to be ordered from a Catholic University in the States.

The messages are quite similar to each other ... each seems to be like a square of mosaic being formed. . . . The messages, given monthly, are meant for the whole world. They are simple but profound.

JANUARY 1986:

"Dear Children: Again I invite you to prayer of the heart. If you pray from your heart, Dear Children, the ice cold hearts of your brothers will be melted and every barrier will disappear. Conversion will be easily achieved by those who want it. You must intercede for this gift for your neighbors."

FEBRUARY 1986:

"Dear Children: This Lent is a special incentive for you to change. Start from this moment. Turn off the television and renounce other things that are useless. Dear Children, I am calling you to individual conversion. This time is for you. Thank you for your response to my call."

MARCH 1986:

"I am calling you to an active approach to prayer. You wish to live everything I am telling you, but you do not have results from your efforts because you do not pray. Prayer will be joy. If you begin, it will not be boring, because you will pray out of pure joy. Thank you for your response to my call."

SIXTH DAY IN MEDJUGORJE
(Eighth day of fasting)

I had awakened during the night feeling unusually light. In fact, it felt like I was floating! I remember thinking, "I hope I can float up the mountain!" At 6:30 a.m. I headed out the door for the mountain behind the Church. Climbing this mountain is the "thing to do" for penance. There is a huge cement cross on top that had been constructed by local villagers to represent their strong faith. This cross had apparently been made long before the apparitions began at Medjugorje. People had told me it was hard climbing that hill but everyone was going . . . all ages and even the crippled. Everyone had their own experience, of course, and worked out something in their own mind. I had heard of a woman being healed of her cancer on the climb.

The path was very rocky . . . people were stopping at each of the twelve crosses recalling the twelve stations when Jesus was crucified. They read out loud at each cross. I was reminded of my trip to Jerusalem. During the climb the main message I got was a lesson from *A Course in Miracles*: "THERE IS NOTHING TO FEAR." Ah yes, how could I forget? It was not that I had these fears of my future public life that I had to GET RID OF, it was instead: THERE IS NOTHING TO FEAR ("Stay in present time, Sondra"). It seemed I had to go up the mountain to be reminded of this. When I got to the top, I was stunned to see a man with only one leg who had made it up there right before me. The climb was a fairly difficult one for most people, and I was astonished he had made it. Behind me was a man with a black velvet suit and a tie. I couldn't believe that either, as it was very hot by 8:00 a.m. Even a man nearly blind was coming up.

I had an easier time than most, I believe, because of all my years of Rebirthing. Maybe it was also because I had so much energy from fasting . . . or maybe it was the Holy Spirit. . . . Anyway, I felt like I was floating, just like in my dream.

The cross on that mountain has been seen to disappear. It has also been seen turning, in a pillar of light. Some have seen a bright figure of a woman replace the cross, lasting a few minutes. It was near this cross that the word PEACE was written in the sky.

Obviously the children are not the only ones who have witnessed miraculous events here. People have seen crosses in the sky formed by clouds and doves. There have been many cases of miraculous healings: remission from blindness, cancers, tumors, all sorts of things.

Today in the morning mass, there was talk about what Mary meant by PEACE. It is different, they said, than when the world talks about Peace. The world usually demands that someone else gives us Peace: and by that, new conflicts begin. The Peace that Our Lady asks for is different because you must bring it yourself. The only road to Peace is personal. That was the morning message. In the afternoon, more comments were made about her August 25 message, two days earlier: Mary has invited us to holiness, the world "invited" was stressed. The first step is to say: "I LOVE GOD." We must pray to be given grace to become really holy. We were reminded that she said we should not forget to seek . . . to ask. Mary is ready to give us every thing, they said. We were reminded to start prayer in families. It was pointed out that in the small country of Austria, 300 prayer groups had already begun, all of which had been inspired here.

Today after the afternoon service, the man who had been writing the Pope came up to me with the lady he had been sitting with. They gave me a newsletter, published in the States, called "Miracle at Medjugorje." It was published by a Lutheran Protestant, Wayne Weible[9]

I was very happy to see on paper some of the things I wanted to know, like more information on the "Secrets" the children were being given. I will quote here what it says:

She is to give each seer ten messages or "secrets" of happenings that will occur in the near future. These messages will be visible signs to mankind that the apparitions are real; and that conversion back to God must be started now. When She has stopped appearing to the youths—a time known only by them—a permanent sign will be left at Medjugorje. It will lead to many healings and conversions in the short time left before the messages become reality. Before the visible sign is given to humanity, there will be three warnings to the world. The warnings will be warnings on the earth. Mirjana is one of the visionaries who will witness them. Three days before one of these warnings, she will advise a priest of her choice. After the first warning, the others will follow within a rather brief period of time. There will be a time period for grace and conversion. After the visible sign, those who are still alive will have little time for conversion. For this reason, the Virgin calls for urgent conversion and reconciliation NOW. According to Mirjana, we are close to the events predicted. All six of the visionaries say that the secrets, in substance, affect the whole world (p. 10 of newsletter).

The secrets are actually written on something very special. Both Mirjana and Ivanka received from The Blessed Virgin a piece of material which looks like paper, but it is not paper. Like cloth, but it is not cloth. On this parchment, all ten secrets are written, with the dates, even the minutes. This parchment cannot be destroyed even by fire. Each of these two seers is told by Mary to select a priest to whom they will give the material on which the secrets are written, ten days before the secrets are to happen. The priest will be able to read the message of each secret and will announce it three days before it happens. He will describe the full nature of the secret, its time and even minute and the place. The Priest will not be able to read all ten secrets at once, but just one by one when the time comes for it to be announced.

LAST DAY AT MEDJUGORJE
(Day 7, Ninth day of fasting)

On my last day I deliberately stayed to myself. I wanted to integrate. After church, an American handed me a book which I was grateful for. It was called "The Apparitions of Our Lady at Medjugorje," by Svetozar Kraljevic.[10] I spent a few hours going through this book to see if there was anything I had really missed in this experience.

One thing I found interesting was a description of how the visionaries see the Madonna:

> The visionaries say that they see the Madonna the same way we see people in regular life, that is, in three dimensions. First they see a bright light, from which the Madonna emerges. However, when they are "immersed" in the vision, they do not see, and have no awareness of anything else. They do not react to anything else around them—people moving about, taking photographs, or simply staring. The visions last 2 to 45 minutes, but usually between 5 and 10 minutes. At the end, the Madonna disappears in the light from which she emerged. Sometimes, before the light disappears, the children see images or symbols: the sun, a cross, a heart. The Madonna said the cross is the sign of salvation, the sun shines on us from above, and the heart is the sign of her Son's love. In other words, the sun is life, the cross is salvation, and the heart is the love of Jesus Christ.[11]

The children say that they do not have the words to describe the beauty of the Madonna. Her face is human; but her beauty is divine. The color of her body and the harmony between her figure and her clothing cannot be described or compared with anything we have seen. Her voice, they say, is very pleasant, like beautiful music, and she speaks in perfect Croation.[12]

Here is another account:

The appearance of the Madonna is always preceded by a splendor of light described by the children as 'glowing with holiness.' When she appears, the Madonna wears a white veil, and her gown is not bound at her waist but flows straight down and conceals her feet. Her dress is bright, luminous gray, which the children find hard to describe. A small black curl is seen on the left side of her face. Only on one occasion was Mary dressed differently; on August 15, the Feast of the Assumption. After this apparition, all the children said she was exceptionally beautiful and "dressed in gold"!

The Madonna's complexion is like that of a country girl's of the region: olive in hue with reddish cheeks. Her facial expressions varies, according to stimuli, as do the expressions of people in everyday life. Her expressions range from joy and happiness to sadness and grief. Her hands are raised in an attitude "typical of charismatic prayer."

On certain feast days, such as Christmas, she appears with the Baby Jesus in her arms. On major feast days, she is smiling and joyous; she wears the same clothing, but is more brilliant in appearance.[13]

Scientific and sociological tests, including neuropsychiatric, medicopsychological, somatic, adolescent and young adult profiles, lifestyle characteristics, and intelligence and educational standards, show the children to be absolutely normal and free from all psycho-pathological reactions.[14]

In my last church service at Medjugorje, the Priest talked about how we should glorify God and how we were made in the image and likeness of God. At the end of the sermon, he asked if there was anyone who had had their rosary turn partly to gold. (Bags and bags of rosaries are daily piled on the steps of the rectory to be blessed during the apparitions.) One woman raised her hand. This was fairly common, he said. Some people who had had it happen took their rosary to a goldsmith to have it examined back home. The goldsmith had said it was a very, very ancient gold. . . .

As I was about to leave the church area, a woman approached me, asking where I was from and where I was going after this. When I told her that I was now on my way to India, she lit up. She had read the book *Autobiography of a Yogi*, she said, and she really loved Yogananda.

I could not help but notice that the last person I spoke to in the churchyard of Medjugorje spoke about Babaji's lineage! Perhaps it was a little "closing touch" from Babaji himself. And why not? Babaji and Jesus *are* one. They are one with God. We are one with God. We are one with them. Catholics are even one with Lutherans. Communists are one with non-communists. These communists had certainly been wonderful to me!

I finally had some grapes, some figs and a peach. . . . It was time to go. . . .

*　*　*　*　*

By sharing these experiences in Medjugorje, I hope that I have inspired you to always reach towards an increasing awareness of God in your life. I hope that I have inspired you to want to correct everything in your life that is not working, everything that keeps you from being at Peace. I hope that I have spiritually touched, in some way, the deepest core of your being.

PEACH ON EARTH
AND GOOD WILL TOWARD MEN.

THE INDIA QUEST

India was the Motherland of our race, and Sanskrit the Mother of Europe's languages: She was the Mother of our philosophy: Mother, through the Arabs, of much of our mathematics: Mother, through the Buddha, of the ideals embodied in Christianity: Mother, through the village community, of self-government and democracy. Mother India is in many ways the Mother of us all.

—Will Durant

Communion with the Divine Spirit is very profound in a place like India. When you are immersed in the continual devotional life that is common in India, you become absorbed in the Divine. The gurus, saints and yogis of India are so absorbed and saturated with the Divine, that just being in their presence is pure bliss. By doing spiritual practices with them, you can tune into their energy field. You can have a transmission of their energy and you can see the full potential of what is possible. It is wonderful to have examples of totally realized beings around. You get intoxicated with their bliss; you get purified and your heart melts.

If you want to be Saint-like (which is, to me, the whole point in life, i.e., "self mastery"), then it helps to be with the Saints and find out what they are like. In 1988 I took 75 students with me and they said it was the highlight of their spiritual lives. Our destination was the two ashrams of Sri Babaji, one in Haidakhan in the foot-hills of the Himalayas and the other higher up into the Himalayas where the Divine Mother Festival is cele-brated. (Babaji once told us that one day there was equivalent to *twelve years* of clearing your karma on the outside—so we are talking about something that is re-ally a major peak experience.)

Babaji is a Mahavatar, which means he is not born of a woman, but instead manifests himself at will. Babaji is a physical manifestation of Lord Shiva, the supreme manifestation of the Divine, according to the Sanatana Dharma. The Sanatana Dharma is not connected with any particular creed or religious tradition. It includes all methods of approaching God through purification and spiritual uplift.[15] Sanatana Dharma can be described as an underlying timeless law for everything created in the universe. It is the absolute truth—a blueprint for every-thing created—the original structure. It is said that every deviation from this original divine law leads to the disso-lution of the creative process and decline of creation.

When righteousness is weak and there is great up-heaval, avatars like Babaji always appear to help support humanity. Babaji first appeared as a ball of light in June 1970. He spent most of his period in a cave near the Gan-ges at Haidakhan. He sat motionless for 45 days without eating, sleeping or drinking.

There are also earlier known manifestations of Shri Babaji. One was from 1800 to 1922. In that form, called "Old Hherakhan Baba," he readily performed miracles, brought people back to life, appeared in several places at once, and was once seen sitting in the center of four fires. He eventually dematerialized his body in 1922.

Some people are afraid that having a guru means you have to give your power away and be subject to his every whim. That is not at all what having a true guru is like. That is what being in a cult may be like. Having a true spiritual master is being connected to a *wondrous* power. The guru transfers spiritual power (shakti) to the pupil and gives him as much as he can take. The pupil learns to become a guru himself. He develops the ability to achieve what would otherwise be far beyond his capacity. The guru gives out teachings according to the capacity and state of preparation of the pupil. The type of guidance the teacher uses varies and is a secret between the teacher and the pupil. Guru means "through darkness to light." A guru is a teacher who by the example of his own purity and Divine being can guide his devotees to truth and the realization of God.[16] A guru can show you and help you experience what Inner Communion really is. A guru is the great realizer of truth and helps transform the existing culture.

Paramahansa Yogananda, an Indian yogi well known in the West, describes Shri Babaji in his book *Autobiography of a Yogi* (Chapters 33 & 34). Babaji was his guru's guru's guru. You can read about Babaji in that book, plus in my recent book called *Pure Joy*, as well as in *Babaji, Shri Haidakhan Wale Baba*, by Gunnel Minett. There is another book called *Haidakhan Baba, Known & Unknown*[17] that I recommend.

When you step on Indian soil, you tend to immediately experience what I call the "collapse of the Western

Mind." I consider this is a very healthy thing, since we tend to be stuck in a limited disposition of Western science and materialism, which tends to deny the Spirit. (The East, as Bubba Free John puts it, tends to deny the world too much and perhaps they need to get that balance from us.) Anyway, there is a tremendous value in experiencing other cultures; you are freed of habitual ways of thinking and rigid belief systems. When the rigid belief systems are uprooted, what is left is more pure aliveness and pure spirit.

This is one of the benefits of going on a quest to India. I have found that it is much easier to go with a group so that you can have the spiritual support and love of the others. The groups I take are unique in that everyone has taken basic trainings such as the LRT (Loving Relationship Training) and has had sufficient Rebirthing experience beforehand. This enables one to have an easier time and be more open to the Communion that is available. And since I take care to rebirth the group every few days with my assistants team, the group is able to maintain better health and stay a lot clearer. The Yogis and Saints have been impressed with the strength and fortitude of the groups that have come along with me.

We always spend a few days in New Delhi, getting used to the culture and shopping for Indian clothes and things needed in the ashram. This past year I was even able to get air-conditioned buses for the long trip up into the mountains (which can take twelve or more hours depending on the condition of the weather and roads). This year when we finally got to Haldwani, we were greeted with the good news that the river was low enough that we would be able to hike into the ashram via the "river route." (Other years the water was too high and we had to hike in on the "jungle route," which takes about four hours and is a lot tougher.) Going the river route is always a lot of fun as one gets to cross the Ganges approximately eight times, either ankle deep, knee deep, waist deep or chest deep, depending on how recent there were monsoons. Since it is quite swift, human "chains" of four people with arms straight out, hands shoulder to shoulder, are necessary to maintain balance. The deeper places are tricky and one must tie one's money belt, containing money, plane tickets and passport, around one's neck, hopefully wrapped in plastic in case you fall in.

This past year we only had a few fall in; but all in all it was great fun, and everyone got incredibly high getting cleansed in the river. By the time we got to Haidakhan most of us felt ourselves in a kind of altered state. When the group saw the temples, many broke down in tears of joy. One cannot really explain the feeling except to say that Haidakhan itself is *pure bliss*. We all felt that. Every year it is a totally different experience. I can only say that this past year the group had many miracles occur . . . major healings, in a few days, of conditions that they had wrestled with for years.

We also had very mystical things occur such as unusual darshans from Babaji. Once he appeared in the sky over the building where I was rebirthing the group. (This was witnessed by three different people, two from my group.) Another time two students in my group saw the murti (living statue) turn to gold and Babaji manifested in a youthful form. One night a woman in our group from New Zealand was out under the stars praying to Babaji and asking him if she should start a healing center in Auckland that she was considering calling "The Phoenix." In a flash she saw a group of stars turn into a Phoenix! She got her answer quite dramatically.

Everyone has their own personal experience of the ashram. Although Babaji is not now regularly physically present there, his essence is everywhere and in everyone. He is actually omnipresent. He can take any form at will. He can appear and disappear anytime he wishes and can communicate telepathically any time, night or day. His main teachings are love, truth, simplicity, and the mantra . . . along with karma yoga and service to mankind.

At the ashram, we spend a lot of time purifying ourselves by chanting in the temple, which is one of the most effective ways of having communion with God. The main mantra we use there is Om Namaha Shivaya. Babaji said it is the ultimate mantra and its effectiveness is unlimited. It can give you the greatest possible happiness, and the power of pure divinity is activated. We also routinely do karma yoga, work dedicated to God in the form of service, which helps us realize that work is worship.

One of the wonderful benefits of Haidakhan is the opportunity to go into the cave and meditate. This past year I took everyone in the cave in groups of five and each group meditated for ten minutes. This cave is mentioned in the Shiva Puran and is described as a resort of gods and a place where Lord Shiva used to meditate. Being inside this cave, described in the Vedas, is always one of the highlights of any trip to Haidakhan. People have had visions, healings, moments of total creativity, past life releases, and all kinds of unusual experiences in there.

Every morning and afternoon everyone bathes in the river to cleanse the body and soul. The river Gautama Ganga is considered very holy and purifying. The river divides the grounds of the Ashram. The main temple is on one side, the cave on the other side. Every morning and evening the Aarti is performed in the temple. This is a beautiful ritual which includes offering fire, flowers, water and fruits along with beautiful devotional chanting.

On this past trip, many cried upon having to leave the lower ashram; however, it was time to go on to the upper ashram and celebrate the Divine Mother Festival. Here we were greeted by more people from all over the world. Everything is intensified and the ceremonies are longer and more elaborate. I have only attended the Divine Mother Festival for the last three years, and even now I feel unable to really write about it in a way that does it justice. I barely integrate it, and it is time to go back. One of the main blessings we have there is being able to be close to Muniraj and Shastriji; Babaji has described them as "two of the purest beings on earth."

PART III

COMMUNION WITH THE GREAT TRADITION

GREAT TRADITIONS

*P*eople may wonder how I can write about such "Christian" issues and yet be so immersed in the teachings of my Indian guru. Some may wonder how I have resolved my very Lutheran background with the fact that I had such a deep experience of the Virgin Mary in a Catholic setting in Yugoslavia. One might assume that all this jumbled together could only cause confusion and chaos, not communion. And yet for me, the truth is that I am a lot less confused now than I was when I was told there was only one way (i.e., the organized religion I grew up with). Only by studying and experiencing many different teachings and traditions was I able to become clear and centered in a real spiritual life that worked for me.

I remember when I first met my master, Babaji, my mother found it very threatening and thought that I had somehow left Jesus. I tried to explain to her that there was no separation, and that I don't have to leave one friend to have another, nor leave one teacher to have another. I could tell she was still very suspicious; but I refused to argue with her about religion. I left for India, where I shaved my head that year. My last day at the ashram, I prayed with fervor to Babaji that I might have a miracle way of getting this across to my mother. That night I had the following vision:

I was trying to rent a new house. The owner told me that the one I liked came complete with a roommate, who was not present right then. But he said I had to decide on the spot if I would take it or not. I wanted the place, so I took my chances about the roommate. The next morning I got up, eager to see who my roommate would be. I looked in the next room. There was Jesus appearing to me full on! It was ecstasy! Later I told my mother this dream-vision and she had no more questions. (She did cry about my head being shaved, but I had to say to her "Mother, you would not deny me one of the most religious experiences of my life, would you?" She let go and finally accepted it.)

I remember as a child when a Catholic family moved into our all Protestant Lutheran community. People were horrified. One of the girls in that family became my best friend, and years later she told me that my dad and grandfather were the only men who spoke to her dad for nearly a year! I was flabbergasted. Religious intolerance must be weeded out forever. It can only be a function of the Ego, not of God, since it is based on separation. Even when I was very little in Sunday School and the teacher would spend hours trying to convince us that our religion was the "right" one, I knew in my little body that that was off . . . but I was not allowed to question anything that was remotely connected to the Bible.

I find that Heart-Master Da Love-Ananda has the most complete and well-expressed statements of any I have ever heard on this subject. I would recommend that everyone study his works. To quote him from the

"Laughing Man Periodical":

> Religious provincialism is the feeling that we are obligated to align ourselves with just one tradition of dogmatic belief, or an exclusively Western (or Eastern) orientation that is ours by virtue of birth, childhood training, or even free choice as an adult. Holding on to our particular belief or orientation, we tend to condemn, disregard, or at best reluctantly tolerate all others. At this point in our cultural history we can maintain these exclusive views only by an act of willful ignorance.
>
> Mankind is in a time of universal communication, interrelatedness, and interdependence. It is no longer appropriate or even possible for individuals, culture or nations to justify absolute independence from other individuals, culture or nations. It is no longer appropriate to grant absolute or ultimately superior status to any historical revelation, belief system or conception of how things work. The entire Great Tradition (the entire mass of traditions) must be accepted as our common inheritance. The secrets of Spiritual process are not contained in the doctrines of any one sect, but are revealed when all are viewed together, as the many arms and legs of a single body of Spiritual Knowledge.[18]

I admire his ability to make this statement so profoundly clear. We all look forward to this work in progress called "Basket of Tolerance." He has in fact dedicated his life to understanding and transcending these differences so that we can comprehend a dynamic great tradition. . . . He goes on to explain that Westerners must be educated in the Eastern traditions and vice versa. He points out that the limited disposition of Western Science denies the Spirit, while the limited disposition of the Eastern view denies the world.[19] He further points out that to live a sacred life, you must be free of all automatic postures and prejudices and habitual ways of adapting the nervous system.

In the *New Teachings* (by Virginia Essene), this is worded yet another way:

> There will never be any code of teaching that will not have to be updated. If we cling to every phrase of the Bible and argue its interpretations, we miss the point. We will not grow as God has intended if we cling to exact working of the holy book. Our interpretations must be expanded. That was a guide for past times.... Church structures must change. We are moving from the age of structure and form to the age of Aquarius, the age of inner knowing ... "See ye first the Kingdom of Heaven Within" was advice we did get 2,000 years ago.
>
> It has been said that the key to survival in the Third Millennium is not competition, but cooperation. Security lies in the Spirit, which is eternal, not in dogma. Offer your life to the Holy Spirit. Ask for guidance. The next thousand years have been labelled by some THE AGE OF PLANETARY AWAKENING. Help everyone. Spread a sense of well-being. Join others. Commune with God and mankind.[20]

Communion and Manifestation

(Considering David Spangler's
The Laws of Manifestation)

*I*t feels right to begin this book with the knowledge of David Spangler and to complete by summarizing, with his permission, an important chapter from his book *The Laws of Manifestation.*[21] It became very clear to me that having and experiencing inner communion would very much transform the way things happened in one's life. As we raise our consciousness to the level in which we are illumined by the light of the indwelling Christ, we will constantly be in a world of absolute wonder. Everything will be easy and joyful and more and more powerful; expansive energies will be constantly coming in. We will function differently, manifest things differently.

The previous way of manifesting things was to use our will with force and perseverance. This would hold in mind a picture to be manifested and visualize it, then project it out in consciousness, the force of will impressing it on the ethers, making it take form and reality. By affirming and visualizing, you reach out and carve out of creation that of which you have need. This has been sufficient. It works.

This method is good for realizing our own power and for learning to be responsible as a creative source. It is very good for a mind still striving for attunement in a world that is under turmoil, bombarded by negative suggestions all around. This method is also good to anchor yourself when you are cleansing yourself of the barnacles of society and the accumulations of your culture which weigh you down. (And it is very important to do this cleansing, or else you will simply become a product of suggestion of society.) Therefore, this method helps you pinpoint your own identity as you release unnecessary cultural programming. One can actually become "weighted down" by excess cultural traditions.

This method also helps you overcome vagueness. It gives you good training in precision. It can also help you to gain peace and security in yourself. It also helps you to center yourself.

The problem is that at a certain point these methods become no longer applicable. They bind you to a level of manipulation of energy that may be too narrow a channel. You can get confined to moving only one step at a time. You may not be providing yourself with the proper power or energy to deal with necessary changes as you invoke higher consciousness. The form that gets manifested may not be most useful for the total need (although it will be useful for the specific need). The manifestation is therefore limited, not free enough to fulfill the whole vision.

In the consciousness of wholeness, complete oneness and total communion, things change. You become at one in the moment with the Spirit and the Light and you become absolutely certain that there is no separation between you and what you want and need. You open yourself without restriction and creation naturally offers you that which will make you even more aware of your wholeness. All things of which you have need are automatically yours. You do not create a mould into which energies must flow, you become the mould. You *know* you are the focal point for all which you have requirement. You draw things to you through absolute *knowing*. (This is *not* a product of the mind, or wishes, or of the heart, it is a product of integrated activity of Being.)

You reach a point where you do not ask. (In the mental level of manifestation, in a sense we see God as a parent, but here we are seeing God as a set of principles.) You do not ask. You know it is there and it is there. God knows your needs even before you ask. The manifestation emerges not only to meet that need, but other ramifications you have been unaware of are met. It is more perfect than you could have even visualized. In fact, full abundance could rush in! But this will not happen until consciousness is so fully expanded that there is no fear of this abundance. No threat. No overwhelm.

And finally, you get higher and higher until you have no needs at all, only perfect fulfillment.

Instant materialization can happen . . . such as materializing an object right out of the ethers. But this requires a consciousness that *knows no limitation* upon itself in terms of need or wondering how needs will be fulfilled. Knowledge and faith must be *absolute* so that it completely identifies with the abundance. (True abundance is not a consciousness of quantity, but rather wholeness, oneness and quality. It is not a consciousness of having everything, but rather of being a source through which that which needs to manifest can manifest.)

Some people, especially religious zealots, may go around saying: "God will supply all my needs ... therefore, I shall simply open myself and allow it to come. I need do nothing." And then they receive nothing. Why? They receive nothing because they are in too much turmoil: they are controlled by subconscious thoughts of a limiting nature that have not been cleared, they are controlled by outside patterns, they are not secure, they are not really at peace, they are vague, they are still having thoughts of separation.

There needs to be a transition where you go from one level to another. Nor do you throw out the old methods. The old will have its applications. You just begin to move with the new. You let the Divine process that is seeking to move through and release fullness do that. You welcome the greater levels that await you. You grow and expand into that new consciousness where you are always that union, that communion with God, where you are that fulfillment.

A need is no longer a thing that fulfills a lack, but rather something that permits and nourishes in the moment the externalization and growth of the God within. You become an example of consciousness *not struggling* with its environment, not fearful, not striving to draw out needs, but a consciousness that is one with the Beloved, the Source, the Source being seen first. You are creative spirit, being itself, inspiring Faith. Perfection unfolds from you. You are a blessing. ... Thank you, David!

Other Quotations on Communion

"The Truth that is God and Life is sufficient in and of itself. We are not separate from that. We are happy only in ecstatic or self-released Communion with That. To release the entire body-mind into Communion with the Radiant and unknowable Divine Reality IS happiness. It is not that the act of such release produces effects in us that are happiness. Rather, the sacrifice or Communion itself, is happiness."[22]

"If you spend time in the company of what is lovable, then the emotional radiance of being will naturally come forward. Right association is the secret then. It is said that of all the things a person can do, association with the God-Realized personality, the saint, the Spiritual Master, is the best; simply to be in the company of one who is lovable in the highest sense, one in love with whom the very Force of God is encountered. The best Company in which to spend all of your time is the Company of God and the Spiritual Master. The practice of heartfelt devotion to God in relationship to the Spiritual Master is the true and Perfect Way of Life. True Religion is simply a matter of maintaining association with God and with the Spiritual Master moment to moment. Recite the names of God, remember God constantly, hold the image of the Spiritual Master, praise the Spiritual Master and think of the Spiritual Master."[23]

"You must serve the Spiritual Master and serve God. You must perform this service with your life—and you must learn how to do it in the form of all your activities so that every action is GOD-COMMUNION. Live on Grace."[24]

"Entering into pleasurable Communion with God is part of our necessary consideration of sexuality. Surrender to God is more pleasurable that sexual play. God-Communion is the primary bodily pleasure. It is simply that you have not realized it as such, and therefore you conceive of God-Communion as self-limiting and ascetic."[25]

"You need not renounce sex if you can fulfill it in love as sexual communion. But it will never be sexual communion if you remain a lustful personality, a self-possessed personality. Lust cannot be coincident with God-Communion. Your lustfulness prevents you from being elegant. It makes you continue to be ordinary and mediocre. but to be free of lust is not to be asexual."[26]

"Let your whole body be converted. This is the greatest Yoga, the foundation yoga of Divine Communion."[27]

"You can practice this Communion only by transcending fear. You must renounce your fear and eliminate conflicts."[28]

"The Way of Divine Communion is to breathe, sur-

114

rendering with every breath into the Life-Principle with unobstructed, radiant feeling, rather than contracted feeling."[29]

QUOTATIONS FROM
A COURSE IN MIRACLES
ABOUT COMMUNION

"The ego uses the body for attack, for pleasure and for pride. The insanity of this perception makes it a fearful one indeed. The Holy Spirit sees the body only as a means of communication, and because communication is sharing, it becomes COMMUNION."[30]

"The Escape from Darkness involves the recognition that there is nothing you want to hide even if you could. This step brings escape from fear. When you have become willing to hide nothing, you will not only be willing to enter in COMMUNION, but will also understand peace and joy."[31]

"The mind we share is shared by all our brothers, and as we see them truly, they will be healed. Let your mind shine with mine upon their minds, and by our gratitude to them make them aware of the light in them. This light will shine back on you and on the whole Sonship. This is true communion with the Holy Spirit, Who sees the altar of God in everyone, and by bringing it to your appreciation, He calls upon you to love God and His creation. You can appreciate the Sonship only as one."[32]

"The miracle sets reality where it belongs. Reality belongs only to Spirit, and the miracle acknowledges only truth. It thus dispels illusions about yourself, and puts you in communion with yourself and God. The miracle joins in the Atonement by placing the mind in the service of the Holy Spirit."[33]

"As long as perception lasts, prayer has a place. Since perceptions rest on lack, those who perceive have not totally accepted the Atonement and given themselves over to truth. Perception is based on the separated state. COMMUNION, not prayer, is the natural state of those who know."[34]

PART IV

CLOSING

A Tribute to the Divine Mother

by Harigovind

"JAI MAHAMAYA KI JAI"
(Hail to the great universal creative energy)

A very dear friend of mine was crossing Germany by foot during the Second World War. One day she found herself in the situation where a Russian soldier entered the room in which she had taken shelter. He was ready to rape her. Instead of going into fear and terror, she stood calmly sending her prayers to Mother Maria. The soldier stood immobilized for a while; then he suddenly sank onto his knees and burst into tears and begged for forgiveness. What happened? Remembering the Mother changed his entire behavior. Perhaps he also remembered his own mother.

We must not only recognize God in the Father form, nor only in the form of the "Mother of God" as Mary. We must come to recognize the Divine Mother herself in all Her forms. The Divine Mother unifies and diversifies. She is the one in the unfolded universe and the universe is one in her. She is the one substance which is the substratum of every communication, of every creation, of every display of power and beauty. She is the one every artist strives for as the transcendent expression of his art. She is the one every businessman strives for in his success and is the one who shines in every human heart when in love. She is the one who perfects science, the Great Inspiratrix who gives the light of knowledge to the minds of leading scientists. She is the origin of consciousness, of all the elements, of all the laws of physics, mathematics, music, economics, languages. She is the primordial cause of all existence, and is eternally one with Shiva, the simple Father.

To speak about Her is courageous and perhaps foolish at the same time; because She can never be fully reached with words, yet She is the Mother of letters and language which She pervades. To write about the Divine Mother resembles the attempt to empty the ocean with a teacup. For She is omnipotent, omnipresent and omniscient. In Her the infinite potentiality is slumbering, to be evolved into the screens of time and space according to Her will.

The Mother is Supreme. She encompasses all opposites and transcends them all. She is supreme power, supreme wisdom, supreme peace, the supreme of the supreme. Name Her electricity, name Her gravity, name Her space. We have learned to use them all, but can we create their existence? Can we create even the smallest flower or the most modest moss?

To have the blessing of Her sight, the saints and scientists of all ages have undergone great penance. In order for the blindness of our inner eye to be lifted, we have to pray to Her with the full power of our heart.

All mankind is striving for happiness . . . but lasting happiness can be found only in true knowledge, and true knowledge implies the knowledge of the Divine Mother.

The "Father oriented" western mind has created the technological civilization to be highly developed. But the feeling side, the inner connection with the matrix, creatrix, the life-giving spring of inner certainty and intuition has nearly been lost. On the other hand, in the eastern cultures, mainly India, the mystic participation in the great life of the Mother has never been lost. However, the skill to handle the scientific technological aspects of modern life has not been developed.

In the West, the absence of the Divine Mother in image and experience resulted in our orientation becoming lopsided and out of balance. There is no difficulty in seeing proof of that in the massive threat of nuclear war, pollution and destruction of the forests. The real solution to all these problems can lie only in a shift of consciousness, in a reorientation of the mind in the same manner as the Russian soldier woke up from his dream. A new orientation to the Divine Mother's energy, a tuning into a higher wisdom is needed. It can be revealed to us through prayer and meditation, as we are all children of one Mother.

"O MOTHER OF BLISS, THOU FILLEST ME WITH SUPREME JOY. THY MERCY IS BOUNDLESS, O MOTHER. FOREVER I BOW TO THEE. TEACH ME. TEACH ME HOW TO BE MORE LOVING. TEACH ME HOW TO BE A CARETAKER OF THIS PLANET."

Closing

The word "Communion" has been traditionally applied to a particular ceremony in the Christian Church. I have attempted to share other meanings and some of my attempts to experience communion during my travels to holy places. But perhaps any moment of quiet within, any moment of true attunement to the light and presence of love, can be called Communion. You can enter that experience of deep reverence and feel the Christ Spirit in your heart. That is the place of true communion: the temple of the heart.

In traditional Christian Communion, you take the bread and the wine with the purpose of stimulating Christ Consciousness. But how can we all stimulate Christ Consciousness more and more and more, even when not having that ceremony? Isn't that the real question?

In his book *Jesus, Teacher and Healer*,[35] White Eagle points out that the bread is the symbol of the cosmic body of Christ which is everywhere and for everyone to take and to eat thereof. He states that we can also absorb into our being the bread of life when we live in service to our brother man. We can partake of the bread of communion by our kind service in the world, by our sincere brotherhood.[36]

The cup, he says, symbolizes the heart and the wine the sweet essence of spirit born of human experience. (We should think of the Outpouring which touches all ... the many in the One and One in the many.) The blood is the life force of the Great Healer, Lord Christ.[37]

Inner Communion is when you keep the Wine and Blood of Christ in your own inner sanctuary. This can be done through the spiritual life; i.e., not only through spiritual practices, but by remembering that all of life is an ashram and every moment is a spiritual opportunity. Pray to be purified by the Divine Love of The Christ. Meditate on this verse: "Be Ye Perfect even as your Father which is in Heaven is Perfect." Create the perfect life on earth by recognizing and knowing you are made perfect. You are one with God the Father.

Christ is light and life and perfection. You are one with that perfection. Raise your consciousness and partake in the bread of life, knowing that you can even become so pure that you can master the very atoms which cause decay of the body and death. You can overcome the last enemy, death! You can truly be sustained by the bread of life, the wine of life. Give thanks for the Eternal Spirit that you are made of. (Your body is not just a "vehicle" for Spirit, it is made of the very substance of eternal Spirit, Spirit being that which cannot be destroyed.) You *are* one with Spirit in Holy Communion; and when you know that and remember that, and claim that, then you are one with Life Itself.

PRAYER: *Oh Great Spirit, may we always be totally in communion with You. May we all cease to think that we are separate from You, that our bodies are separate from You. May we always be partaking of the bread and wine of life that You offer us. May we always be abiding in Love and Christ Consciousness at all times. May we always be in Holy Communion with You and Man.*

CLOSING PRAYERS

I acknowledge the presence of the Holy Spirit in me. I welcome more of this presence into my life.

I ask for the Intelligence of Christ Consciousness.

I welcome the Christ and the Holy Spirit into my affairs.

I pray for direction.

Let me be spiritually fit to survive.

May we as a Nation, welcome and acknowledge the Spirit.

May we experience Inner Communion with the Great Spirit and be Blessed with Wisdom.

APPENDIX

Communion by Floating

This may seem like an odd title for a chapter; however, I have recently seen the immense value of entering other states of being (communion) by deliberately putting myself in an environment that can give a rich, elaborate state of inner experience quickly. The environment I am speaking of is a Floatation Tank. I have discussed the most common techniques I use, such as rebirthing and chanting, etc. But for variety and experimentation I recommend you try the "float to relax" experience. This entails floating atop ten-inches of water in a dark enclosed chamber. The theory is that when one or more senses are restricted, the sensitivity of other senses is expanded. A float tank can be one of the best investments one could make, as it has been said that floating:

* "results in a spontaneous reduction and/or elimination of such habits as smoking, drinking and drug abuse;

* lowers the levels of biochemicals directly related to stress, anxiety and tension;

* gives the floater access to unusual powers of creativity, imagination, visualization, and problem-solving;

* helps athletes to improve their performance significantly;
* enhances superlearning by increasing the mind's powers of comprehension, retention and original thinking;
* gives the floater in two hours more rest and restoration than a full night of sound sleep."[38]

Besides all this, what I am very interested in are the life-enhancing effects and the potential for spiritual revelation.

I have found that in order for me to reach deep levels of meditation, it can take effort. But in the tank, with the elimination of all distractions, I am able to go, almost immediately, into deep meditation. I feel a deep sense of harmony and a euphoric feeling of "inner communion." I have actually received vivid instructions from the Divine, and have heard voices and seen apparitions while in the tank. These experiences were never scary; in fact they were natural and extremely valuable.

Apparently, the release from gravity allows the blood to circulate more freely and completely, reaching parts of the body that need healing. There is research that seems to prove that floating increases the production of Theta waves. This is a mysterious state, which is potentially highly productive and enlightening. It seems to take Zen monks some twenty years to be able to generate this state at will.[39] It has also been proven that a synchronization and balancing of brain hemispheres takes place during floatation. This gives a feeling of unity, harmony and wholeness.

All in all, one does experience a unique state of being,

which is extraordinarily quiet and intensely conscious. The effects, for me anyway, go beyond meditation or simply relaxing in a quiet room. Other techniques require discipline and dedication. This could be the Lazy Man's way. It is quite literally effortless. So for those of you who have resisted the other methods I have suggested, why not give this a try?

SUPERSPACE

The latest development in "float tanks" is Super-Space. Now you can stay *dry* and cozy through the whole floatation experience! Neither salt nor water ever touch you. You don't need showers before or after. You can jump in without ever taking your clothes off; and you get all the benefits of floating, because the salt water is enclosed in a special mattress. The SuperSpace Relaxer I tried was in Denver, Colorado. I only had a fifteen-minute test experience, and I was very impressed. I went into a very deep communion and state of meditation that I find difficult to get into otherwise. There is also a special listening environment, allowing for super-learning and self-programming tapes; and even SyberVision for undisturbed private viewing. It can also be turned into a biofeedback device. There is airflow and climate control; and besides, the unit is very beautiful.

It seemed perfect to me for deep relaxation, contemplation, visualization and exploration of creative states of mind. These new SuperSpace units are also being used for accelerated learning, rehearsal of athletic activity for enhanced performance, stress reduction, body-centered therapy, addiction recovery programs, pain relief and extraordinary comfort and rest or sleep during pregnancy, post-op and other medical conditions.

You float in approximately nine inches of salt water. A loose membrane of flexible strong material, covered by a sheet, conforms to the surface of your skin and keeps you dry. The salt water supports you evenly. You are dry; but the sensation is very much like floating in a lake on your back, side or stomach. It feels wonderful.

Really, it is like a warm modern *cave* where you may come to know yourself.[40]

A Society in Communion:
The Dream People

Reprinted from *Maggie's Farm*,
Alternative Network Magazine
Issue No. 36, 1987

Deep in the mist-shrouded jungle of the Central Malaysian highlands live the extraordinary *Senoi*—the Dream People.

The *Senoi* Tribe are a unique and remarkable culture that have puzzled anthropologists since the 1930s. They are totally non-violent people. They have no number system, written language, or technology yet have amazed scientists with their high level of mental and social sophistication, emotional well-being and an almost total lack of violence.

These remarkable people are masters of what we would call in the West, "conflict resolution." Their secret is somehow linked to the fact that Senoi daily life is based entirely upon their dreams. Almost from the time a Senoi child can talk they are taught how to dream, how to project into their dream life to master the forces their dreams reveal. . . .

Dreams lie at the very heart of Senoi inspiration and faith, for they believe that dreams reveal a deeper reality, a "spirit world" from which the events we experience originate. Senoi parents encourage their children to travel to specific locations in their dreams—such as a nearby pool of forest—to see if fishing or hunting will be good there the next day.

The children are urged to project their souls beyond the normal boundaries, for they believe this is what makes a person charismatic and strong. Fear, on the other hand, drives a person's soul deeper into the body, a condition the Senoi say is unhealthy and conducive to illness. The Senoi teach their children to release pent-up fears through their dreams. They appear to use their dreaming as an "emotional safety valve." They say that anything experienced in a dream can be an asset or a liability, depending on whether the dreamer is wise enough to know how to use it.

The extensive dream education Senoi children receive in their early years has produced a society in which dreams are central to much adult interaction. Dreams are discussed as an important consideration at Village Councils, and decisions as to which land should be planted when, are not made until time has been allowed to dream on it.

... Almost all Senoi art, including music, dance routines and decorative patterns, are dream-inspired, as is Senoi religion. Children are anticipated and named from dreams. Dreams play a very important part in the diagnosis and treatment of disease. It is even said that occasionally a young man will first meet his wife in a dream, and that once he knows who and where she is, will travel to a distant valley to locate his dream girl!

The Senoi are "animists" who believe that everything

in the teeming jungle around them has a living spiritual essence. They don't see themselves as *generators* of consciousness as we do in the West, but rather as *channels* of a vital essence that is far greater than any individual. Consciousness is seen as more fundamental than time, space or matter. And the basis of this belief is the real evidence of dreams, for dreams can often reveal a glimpse of the future or an event too distant to be known by normal means.

. . . Perhaps the most striking feature of the Senoi is their shyness. Senoi simply means "people," and anthropologists believe they are the last remnants of a sophisticated ancient culture that once extended throughout much of Southeast Asia but was pressed into the deep jungles of the mountainous interior by the invasions of more technologically advanced and aggressive people.

The Senoi are an extremely gentle people who abhor violence and take great pride in saying: "We never get angry, only MAI (outsiders) get angry." They try to avoid outsiders and confrontation, retreating deeper and deeper into the jungle to dream.

Because almost no violence or crime has existed within their culture, the Senoi have never found it necessary to create a system of authority. Any disputes (usually over women) are heard by a selected group to settle the matter as quickly and quietly as possible. The only traditional idea of rank is the title of "TOHAT" or healer. Senoi children do not take part in competitive games, but wrestle and play as children anywhere do.

Researchers believe that the extraordinary psychological balance that characterizes Senoi society results from the fact that the people are raised to appreciate elemental and psychological forces that dreams reveal. The lack of friction within Senoi society is attributed to their technique of dissipating social tension in their dreams rather than projecting it onto others in waking hours.

While the Senoi are uncommonly gentle during their waking hours, they believe that violence in dreams is not bad—for only by killing the images that cause terror can they destroy their power to do harm. Psychological data from various groups reveal a consistent ability to conquer "dream enemies" and find "treasures" in their dreams.

. . . Adolescent Senoi learn to tap the "power" of their dreams by developing deep, life-long relationships with the "spirits" they encounter while dreaming—which they all "GURAG," or dream-helpers. The "GURAG" are seen as teachers and give the Senoi gifts of songs, dances and special powers.

Senoi dream practices work on the principle that, during our waking hours, we create images of people and objects we see around us. Through their unique appreciation and active use of dreams, the Senoi are constantly aware that, at a certain level of our being, we are intimately connected to everyone and everything we know. The Senoi belief that everything is alive is recognition that the world we perceive is full of our own spirit, and the Senoi realize to a greater extent than most of us that we create the world we experience. Through their dreams the Senoi have found a means of liberating their creative potential, of gaining access to the deepest treasures of the human soul.

Writing this Book

I wrote part of this book in Yugoslavia and finished it in New Zealand on a boat named "Brigand," owned by my friend Briar who took care of me while I wrote. We anchored near the wild islands off the coast, stopping first near Kawaii Island in the bay where Briar was actually conceived on a boat! ("Of course," I thought, "no wonder she is crazy about boating!") The harbors in the area were very gentle and one could see the history of past enterprises ashore: coppermine shafts, gold crushers and whaling equipment.

We spent most of the time near the rugged Great Barrier Island where we rarely saw anyone. It was totally quiet. Most of the time I relaxed and wrote while Briar caught some fresh snapper, mao mao, and trevelli. Occasionally she would take a dingy to shore to walk her dog. Once we visited a small Maori settlement to see if we could buy some crayfish.

When I had to leave to do a seminar in town, I flew out by the sea plane called "SeaBea." It seemed to be a vintage craft that had a very intimate relationship with the sea. As it roared, streams of water flew everywhere and it finally vibrated up, with a sideways maneuver through the mountains.

As I looked down, I was simply astonished, once again, at what New Zealand had done for me. I had had a burst of immense creativity, having not only finished the book, but also I had started a new division of the LRT and actually had manifested a new training called "Evolution" . . . all in a few days! I am forever grateful to this rugged, gentle country, which always takes one somehow by surprise. Beautiful New Zealand, one of the few unspoiled places left, offers so much . . . a real communion with nature and God. It was just the right energy for me to do this book. I offer this as a tribute to the "Kiwis." Thank you!

Endnotes

1. Heart-Master Da Love-Anada, "The Transmission of Happiness," *The Laughing Man.* (The Dawn Horse Press, Vol. 7, No. 1), p.56.

2. Ibid., p. 57.

3. Ibid., p. 19.

4. "A Manual for Teachers," *A Course in Miracles*, p. 83.

5. Summary of "Christmas as the End of Sacrifice," from the "Text," *A Course in Miracles*, pp. 304-306.

6. Sondra Ray, *Pure Joy* (Celestial Arts, 1989).

7. For information about "Immortality Initiation Retreats" with Robert Coon (daily work with R. Coon for one to two weeks) in Glastonbury, write: Robert Coon, c/o Rose Christian, 20 Selwood Road, Glastonbury, Somerset, England.

8. Inspired by an article in *Maggie's Farm, Alternative Network Magazine* (Australia), Issue No. 36, 1987.

9. Order "Miracle at Medjugorje" from Weible Columns, P.O. Box 2647, Myrtle Beach, SC 29478, for $35/thousand, minimum order.

10. Svetozar Kraljevic, *The Apparitions of Our Lady at Medjugorje* (Chicago: Franciscan Herald Press).

11. Ibid., p. 54.

12. Ibid., p. 55.

13. Ibid., pp. 57-58.

14. Ibid., p. 198.

15. Gunnel Minett, *Babaji, Shri Haidakhan Wale Baba*, p. 8.

16. Ibid., p. 13.

17. Baba Hari Dass, *Haidakhan: Known & Unknown* (Davis, CA: Sri Rama Foundation, 1975).

18. Heart-Master Da Love-Ananda, "Creating Access to the Great Tradition: An Introduction to the Basket of Tolerance," *The Laughing Man* (The Dawn Horse Press, Vol. 7, No. 1) , pp. 9-10.

19. Ibid., p. 12.

20. Virginia Essene, *New Teachings for an Awakening Humanity* (Santa Clara, CA: S.E.E. Publishing, 1986).

21. David Spangler, *The Laws of Manifestation* (Moray, Scotland: Findhorn Publications, 1975).

22. Heart-Master Da Love-Ananda, *The Enlightenment of the Whole Body* (The Dawn Horse Press).

23. Heart-Master Da Love-Ananda, *Compulsory Dancing* (The Dawn Horse Press, 1978), p. 43.

24. Ibid., p. 52.

25. Ibid., pp. 58-59.

26. Ibid., pp. 74-75.

27. Ibid., p. 77.

28. Ibid., p. 91.

29. Ibid., p. 97.

30. The "Text," *A Course in Miracles*, p. 97.

31. Ibid., p. 8.

32. Ibid., p. 114.

33. Ibid., p. 9.

34. Ibid., p. 41.

35. White Eagle, *Jesus: Teacher & Healer* (The White Eagle Publishing Trust, British Library CIP Data, Great Britain, Oxford University Press, 1985).

36. Ibid., p. 92.

37. Ibid., p. 93.

38. Michael Hutchinson Quill, *The Book of Floating*.

39. Ibid., p. 16.

40. For information on SuperSpace Relaxers, write to: Samco Development, Inc., 3000 Broadway, Suite 9, Boulder, CO 80302; telephone (303) 938-8738.